Folk Songs

collected by

Ralph Vaughan Williams

edited by Roy Palmer

J M Dent & Sons Ltd
London   Melbourne   Toronto

First published 1983
Selection, introduction, notes © Roy Palmer 1983

This book is set in 11 on 13 Linotron 202 Sabon Roman by
Tradespools Limited, Frome, Somerset
Printed and made in Great Britain by Biddles Ltd, Guildford,
for J. M. Dent & Sons Ltd
Aldine House, 33 Welbeck Street, London W1M 8LX

British Library Cataloguing in Publication Data

Folk songs collected by Ralph Vaughan Williams.
  1. Folk-songs, English
  I. Palmer, Roy
  784.4'942   M1738

ISBN 0–460–04558–X

CONTENTS

[iii]

They have behind them not the imagination of one great poet, but the accumulated emotion, one may almost say, of the many successive generations who have read and learned and themselves fresh re-created the old majesty and loveliness ... There is in them, as it were, the spiritual life-blood of a people.

Gilbert Murray on the Bible and Homer; applied by Vaughan Williams to folk songs (*National Music*, 1934, p. 42)

Introduction

Stories of seeing the light on the Damascus road are always attractive, though not invariably accurate. So far as folk song was concerned, Ralph Vaughan Williams's illumination took place on 4 December, 1903, in an Essex village only twenty miles from London. He was 31 at the time, and beginning to make his name as a composer, but he had been aware of folk songs for many years already. As a child he had been fascinated by a version of 'The Cherry Tree Carol' found in Bramley and Stainer's *Christmas Carols Old and New* (1871). As a young man he familiarised himself with the volumes of folk songs, edited by such collectors as Frank Kidson, Sabine Baring Gould and Lucy Broadwood, which appeared in the 1890s. The Broadwood family, of Lyne, Surrey, was friendly with the Wedgwoods of Leith Hill Place in the same county; and Vaughan Williams's mother was born a Wedgwood, who took her young children back to the family home after the death of her husband. John Broadwood died in 1864, twelve years before Vaughan Williams was born, having published in 1843 the first collection of English folk songs with their tunes. This was re-issued in 1890, augmented by further songs collected by his daughter, Lucy, who published a first volume of her own three years later, under the title of *English County Songs* (with J. A. Fuller-Maitland). Vaughan Williams knew both books well, and when he was invited to give some university extension lectures on folk song in 1902, Lucy Broadwood, drawing on her own collections, sang illustrations for him. However, he felt at that time that he had yet to hear folk songs under their 'native conditions', and he 'believed in them vaguely, just as the layman believes in the facts of astronomy; my faith was not yet active' (*English Folk Songs*, n.d., 1912, p.4). Then came the revelation.

Vaughan Williams was lecturing at Brentwood in the autumn of 1903, when he was approached by two middle-aged ladies, the daughters of the vicar of the neighbouring village of Ingrave. They invited him to attend a tea which their father was giving later in the year for local old people, some of whom might possibly know country songs. 'Though Ralph was rather shy of a Parish Tea', writes Ursula Vaughan Williams, 'and though he felt it most unlikely that anyone there would know any folk songs, he accepted the invitation' (*RVW. A Biography of Ralph Vaughan Williams*, 1964, p.66). No doubt the two ladies did

Vaughan Williams in about 1903
Courtesy of the English Folk Dance & Song Society

some preparation, and Vaughan Williams duly met some singers at the party. On the following day he noted twenty-two songs, seven of them from a seventy-year-old labourer, Mr Charles Pottipher. The first song he sang was 'Bushes and Briars' (no 16), at which Vaughan Williams experienced a deep sense of recognition, as though 'he had known it all his life'. This was a turning point, both in his career as a composer, and in the preservation and subsequent revival of English folk song.

Mainly during the next ten years, Vaughan Williams diligently amassed a collection of 810 songs, together with some singing games and country dance tunes which need not concern us here. Despite having a private income, he was not able to occupy himself exclusively with song collecting, since he was also in the process of making his way as a composer and man of music. However, he devoted as many as thirty days a year to the activity, often at holiday times, sometimes when visiting friends in other parts of the country, such as the Gattys at Hooton Roberts, near Rotherham. He made frequent excursions into Surrey and Sussex with bicycle and notebook; then there were journeys by train, such as the famous expedition to King's Lynn in 1905, when he obtained some thirty songs, including 'The Captain's Apprentice' (no 53), the tune of which recurs in many of his compositions. He found singers at times by strolling into a likely public house, something which Lucy Broadwood envied, because a lady might not do that sort of thing at the time. Friends would recommend likely singers to him: several of his Hampshire informants seem to have been unselfishly given to him by other collectors. In 1911 he went on a short bicycle-mounted tour with fellow-composer George Butterworth, who later died in the First World War, when they noted songs simultaneously from particular singers. Vaughan Williams travelled as far north as Cumberland in the west, Northumberland in the east, and Yorkshire in the middle. In the midlands he visited Derbyshire and Herefordshire, where his contact was Mrs E. M. Leather, whom he met at the Three Choirs Festival. The south-west he avoided altogether. Perhaps distance was a factor; and he certainly knew that Baring Gould had extensively worked Devon and Cornwall and that his friend, Cecil Sharp, was cultivating the county of Somerset. The bulk of his collection came from the south-east and East Anglia, within fairly easy reach of his successive homes in London and his mother's home at Leith Hill Place.

The year 1904 was his *annus mirabilis*, with 234 songs noted – over a quarter of his whole collection. The work went on steadily for some years, then began to fall away. No doubt some of the singers died – they were often very old when Vaughan Williams first met them; and his work as a composer went rapidly forward, partly impelled and considerably influenced by folk song. By 1913, however, his tally of songs had declined to 29, and this was more or less the end of his collecting, which had lasted for ten years. After returning from service in the army during the war, he seems to have made only two more forays in search of song, amassing a total of only sixteen items (three in 1922, and thirteen in 1926, though some of his undated collectanea may date from these years).

Vaughan Williams was fired by 'the beauty and evident antiquity of many of the tunes' (Ursula Vaughan Williams, *op. cit.*, p.70), and by the need to record these ephemeral survivals before they were irretrievably swept away. His predominantly aesthetic attitude, combined with his philosophy of what we would now call rescue archaeology, produced immense riches, but also left him open to certain criticisms, in retrospect, as to his manner of collecting. A modern collector would wish to record every possible item from a singer's repertoire, together with any information, not only about how he or she learned the songs, but also on attitudes to them, views on their meaning and function, and their place in his or her life.

On the whole, Vaughan Williams was more interested in the song than the singer, in the melody than the message. He knew very well that a large number of traditional song texts had been preserved in the form of street ballads, and he preferred to spend the relatively small amount of time at his disposal in attempting to save tunes. Here is his manuscript of 'Bushes and Briars':

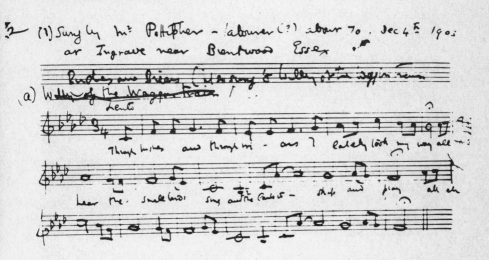

We know that Vaughan Williams completed the text from a Fortey ballad sheet, though it is not clear whether Charles Pottipher knew only the first verse, or whether it was just a question of saving time. Some singers undoubtedly remembered only fragments of songs; in some cases, Vaughan Williams simply could not keep up with them, or could not hear very well, and gaps in manuscripts occurred, or he noted some verses, then wrote: 'unfinished'. After all, he was trying to note melody and variants, and also, in longhand, the words. He was usually alone, though a short expedition with George Butterworth has been mentioned. On one occasion at least, in 1912, he was accompanied by his wife and also Mrs Leather to a hop-picking encampment at Monkland, near Leominster in Herefordshire, to find a singer called Alfred Price Jones. Mrs Leather writes: 'He agreed to sing, so we all sat down on upturned buckets, kindly provided for us by the gypsies, and while Dr Vaughan Williams noted the tune his wife and I took down alternate

Two singers from King's Lynn, James Carter on the left and Mr Anderson in the centre, together with the Rev. Alfred Huddle who probably introduced them to Vaughan Williams.
Courtesy of Mrs Ursula Vaughan Williams

lines of the words' (quoted in L. Jones, *A Nest of Singing Birds*, 1978, p.52). Incidentally, when Vaughan Williams was later asked for his 'most memorable musical impression for the year 1912' he replied that it was 'hearing a gypsy sing at Monkland', and added: 'It was a clear September night and we stood by the blazing fire in the open ground of the gypsy encampment; the fire had been specially lighted to enable us to note down tunes and words in the growing darkness. Then out of the half-light came the sound of a beautiful tenor voice, singing "The Unquiet Grave"' (*ibid*, p.53). The song was published in the *Journal of the Folk Song Society* (vol. VIII, p.102).

As well as helping him to track down singers and to note their words, Mrs Leather also sent texts on to Vaughan Williams: there are several examples of her neat handwriting in his scrapbook. In addition, she recorded songs on phonograph cylinders, and asked him to notate the tunes for her. Several of his transcriptions from her recordings are to be found in her *Folklore of Herefordshire* (1912; reprinted 1970). Skilled as he was in transcribing from the phonograph cylinders, Vaughan Williams, unlike Bartok and Percy Grainger, but like his friend, Cecil Sharp, does not seem to have been fond of the recording machine. Perhaps he was put off by the mechanical difficulties, which were not inconsiderable; perhaps he preferred the immediacy and unobtrusiveness of his notebook and pencil. However, he did record on wax a small number of songs – less than twenty, and even fewer of the cylinders have survived. A total of seven songs (including nos 31, 101 and 110) have been transcribed on to modern tape, and can be heard at Cecil Sharp House. Others may yet come to light.

This still leaves 790 songs which were taken down by hand. Since many tunes were collected at single sessions, it would have been physically difficult to take down all the texts. For example, at one of his meetings with the Sussex *Meistersinger*, Henry Burstow (for whom, see nos 111 to 115), on 22 December, 1904, Vaughan Williams took down sixteen tunes, not one with words. They were: 'Boney's in St Helena' (2), 'Dreams of Napoleon' (5), 'Deeds of Napoleon' (4), 'Grand Conversation of Napoleon' (6), 'The New Deserter' (13), 'Battle of America' (22), 'Green Mossy Banks of the Lee' (8), 'In Essex there lived a rich farmer' (104), 'It's of a sailor now I write' (109), 'Effects of Love' (144), 'New York Street' (153), 'Croppy Boy' (150), 'Peggy Ban' (273), 'Pretty Wench' (245), 'London Apprentice' (181) and 'Gosport Beach' (157). Now, few singers know tunes without words, certainly in such numbers; but Burstow had a cherished repertoire of 420 songs which he was perfectly capable, over a series of evenings, of singing right through, and the numbers in brackets are those in his list, so the words were undoubtedly available.

In fact, Vaughan Williams took down only 237 texts (out of 810 songs in the collection), and many of these were limited to the first verse. He remedied the deficiency to some extent by drawing upon his

Henry Burstow of Horsham, Sussex.
Courtesy of Tony Wales

knowledge of street ballads, as with 'Bushes and Briars'. Occasionally, however, he would spurn words precisely because they were widely printed. For 'Young Henry the Poacher' (no 57), for example, he commented: 'The complete words, which are of no great interest, are on a Such ballad sheet'. Few singers' texts are absolutely identical with printed sheets, and Vaughan Williams must have missed a good deal by way of individual turns of phrase, local vocabulary, and indeed of significant variation. To return to Burstow, after noting from him the tune and first verse of 'Creeping Jane' (no 112), Vaughan Williams broke off with the single word: 'Kidson'. The reference can only be to the text of the song from a Such sheet reprinted by Frank Kidson in the

[xiv]

Journal of the Folk Song Society (vol. I, p.233). It is fortunate that we have Burstow's text, since he wrote it down for Vaughan Williams, together with some others. It has several substantial variations from the Such broadside, such as this:

Such, v.2
When Creeping Jane came on the race-course,
The gentlemen viewed her all round,
And all they had to say concerning Creeping Jane:
'She's not able to gallop o'er the ground'.

Burstow, v.2
It's when that we came to fair Nottingham,
The people all did say:
'Poor Jane is not able to gallop o'er the plain,
And to win the bets that are laid'.

In addition, Burstow's words have the rounded feel of the oral version that they are. It might be argued that these are trivialities, but variation is the lifeblood of folk song.

Considerable numbers of texts, some bound with the manuscripts and some in the scrapbook, are in the handwriting of singers. Vaughan Williams followed the practice of Lucy Broadwood in this respect, and there is no harm in it, except that the singers appear to have been asked to supply only certain texts. The selection seems to have been based on whether the words were 'of interest', and in some cases whether they were deemed to be unduly explicit sexually. Burstow's 'Cheshire Gate' (no 115), fortunately, slipped through the net.

Vaughan Williams was no prude, but when it came to publishing songs he had no choice but to bow to the prevailing taste. So, when he found 'The Cobbler', he published only the tune and first verse in the *Journal*, with the comment: 'The rest of the words are not suitable for publication and have little interest except, perhaps, in giving a modern example of the kind of rough fun which we find in Chaucer's "Clerk of Oxenforde". The words are evidently modern, since a policeman is one of the characters introduced' (vol. II, p.157). At least he took the trouble to preserve the complete song:

The Cobbler
O a story a story to you I will tell
Concerning a butcher in London did dwell
The butcher was possessed of a beautiful wife
And the cobbler he loved her as dear as his life
To my whack fol de lido doodle all the day

Now the cobbler goes to market to purchase an ox   [butcher]
The little cobbler warily as any fox
He slipped on his Sunday clothes and courting he did go
To the jolly butcher's wife because he loved her so

He went unto the butcher's wife 'have you jobs for me'
(O yes ?) says the butcher's wife I will run up to see
She went unto the bedside and gave this snob a call
O I have found an easy job if you have got an awl.

Then up jumps the cobbler and goes for his sharp awl
Then says she 'if you don't be quick you shall not do it at all
But if you do it workmanlike some cash to you I'll pay'
Thank you says the cobbler and began to stitch away

But as the cobbler was at work a rap came at the door
The cobbler crawled beneath the bed and lay upon the floor
O lay still says the butcher's wife, what will my husband say
– Then she let a policeman in along with her to play

The butcher came from market he put them in a fright
The policeman scrambled downstairs and soon got out of sight
And the butcher's wife so nimble she locked the bedroom door
But in her fright she quite forgot the cobbler on the floor

The butcher gets indoors and he went upstairs to bed
There's something here is very hard the butcher smiled and said
His wife said it is my rolling pin the butcher could but laugh
'How came you now to roll your dough with a policeman's staff'.

The butcher threw the weapon underneath the bed
There he broke the chamber pot and cracked the cobbler's head
The cobbler called out murder cries the butcher 'Who are you'
'I am the little cobbler that mends the ladies' shoes'

Then if you are the cobbler come along with me
I'll pay you out for mending shoes before I'm done with thee
He locked him up in the bull's bed – the bull began to roar
There the butcher laughed to see him (?) tumbling o'er and o'er

It was early next morning when the people were about
The butcher rubbed his face with blood and turned the cobbler out
He pinned a paper on his back and on it was the news
The cobbler in the bedroom goes to mend the ladies' shoes

The people all seemed frightened and home this cobbler run
His cotton britches were so torn that here he shewed his bum
His wife she stood staring, he knocked her on the floor
And says you brute I'll never go out a-mending any more

[xvi]

At least Vaughan Williams did not re-write or bowdlerize for publication, but at times he committed the cardinal sin of not preserving, even in manuscript, the words of a song which he judged unfit for print. One example is 'The Long Whip', published with the comment: 'The rest of the words are not suitable for this journal' (vol. II, p.207):

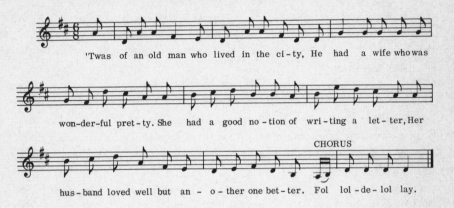

'Twas of an old man who lived in the ci-ty, He had a wife who was won-der-ful pret-ty. She had a good no-tion of wri-ting a let-ter, Her hus-band loved well but an - o - ther one bet-ter. Fol lol -de- lol lay.

As the printed version, so the manuscript, and Vaughan Williams noted no more words for this intriguing song. To his credit, he confessed to A. L. Lloyd, many years later, that he had long regretted his omission in this case. Alas, the song appears to be now lost. I have hunted high and low without finding either a broadside text or an analogous version from oral tradition.

Perhaps because of his desire to rescue interesting songs, and especially their tunes, from oblivion, Vaughan Williams did not attempt to explore singers' repertoires in full, nor even to identify all his informants. Of the 248 singers represented in his collection, 52 are anonymous, listed for example as 'man from Stepney' (no 81), 'gypsy' (nos 120 and 121) or merely 'singer' (nos 13 to 15). It was not always possible for him to obtain the names of singers across a crowded taproom or in a hop-field, and he appears to have done his best to note them. He often omits occupations, but those listed are invariably working class, and predominantly rural: labourer, woodcutter, bricklayer, fisherman, sailor, carter, sailmaker, shepherd, cowman, shoemaker, sexton, tailor, publican. In some cases, all too few, he has information on where singers learned their songs, and where they sang them.

Thus he says of the songs, including 'Died for Love' (*Journal*, vol. II, p.159), sung by an unnamed 'servant at Ingrave Rectory' that 'she learnt them at home (Chigwell) where they often used to have the neighbours come in and sing in the evening' (MS 8vo A, p.1). Another of his Ingrave singers, Mrs Humphrys, had one song, 'Adieu to Old England' from her grandfather (MS II, p.102), another, 'The Cambric Shirt' (no 18) from her father, and a third, 'The Golden Glove' (no 17) from her grandmother, 'Ann Smyth, born in 1794 at Blackmore, Essex ... Her parents, husband and children's husbands were all Essex villagers'. Mr Stacey, who sang to Vaughan Williams at Hollycombe, Sussex, in 1904, was a cowman aged about 80 who 'learnt most of them [his songs; see nos 98 and 99] from his father. He and a friend used to go wassailing – he used to know about 50 songs. He used the expression "outway"' (MS II, p.166). Mr Stephen Poll, of Tilney St Laurence, Norfolk, was another 80-year-old labourer who not only sang, but played dance tunes on the fiddle: 'He learnt the dances at Lynn Fair. He used to fiddle for dances – the old country dances made more money for him because each couple as they got to the top gave him a penny' (MS III, p.118). Mr Jake Willis (for whom, see nos 83–85) was 'a veteran of the Crimean War and the Indian Mutiny'. Mr Knaggs (see no 118) 'was sexton of Westerdale and played the "bass fiddle". I found it difficult to take down the words as they were [he admitted] "broad Yorkshire"' (MS III, p.7). A Surrey man, Mr Earle (see no 89), was a labourer, aged 61 in 1904, who learned most of his songs 'off "ballets" or from his father'.

Notes like this occur in only a few cases, and are interesting but tantalisingly brief; so many questions remain unanswered. What were the rest of Mr Stacey's fifty songs, since Vaughan Williams took down only five? Where did Mr Poll learn to play the fiddle? Did Mr Willis learn his songs at home or in the army? If the latter, were they sung in the Crimea and India, and on what occasions? Where did Mr Earle buy his 'ballets' (street ballads), and where did he find the tunes to put to them? One could multiply such questions, for these and for other singers, and ideally one would like to have their full life histories. All this would be a very tall order indeed for Vaughan Williams's 248 singers, but even if only a few of his major informants had been interviewed in depth it would have been immensely valuable. Only one of them, Henry Burstow, has left an autobiography (*Reminiscences of Horsham*, 1911).

There was undoubtedly a gulf between the middle-class song collectors who were at work in the twenty-five years or so before the First World War and their working-class informants, and it has recently been suggested that the collectors exploited the singers, merely snatching their songs and running. In addition, it is argued that they wrenched the songs out of context, out of the background from which they sprang. This may have a grain of truth, but seems on the whole unfair. If people like Vaughan Williams had not collected these songs, many would have disappeared, leaving us immeasurably the poorer. In the second place, Vaughan Williams, and many of his fellow-collectors, for that matter, had a deep respect and affection for their informants. Vaughan Williams spent a great deal of time and effort in visiting singers, some of them repeatedly. On at least one occasion, however, in March, 1904, three men appeared by his window in Westminster: 'Ralph was delighted to hear ballad singers in Barton Street. He bought copies of all the broadsheets they had, and took down another song, "William and Phyllis", which they sang for him' (Ursula Vaughan Williams, *op.cit.*, p.67. The ballad sheets were preserved in his scrapbook, and the song published in the *Journal*, vol. II, p.216–7). Again, in the summer of 1908, 'one evening in Ledbury he heard a girl singing a ballad to two men. The pubs were just closing and these three, standing in the road outside in the light of the still open door, looked like a group in a story' (*ibid*, p.83). Vaughan Williams asked for other songs, and was referred to the parents of one of the men. He visited them the following day, but found they 'had no songs worth collecting, although he found some among their neighbours' (*ibid*, p.84. There is no trace of the ballad from Ledbury in the manuscripts, but Vaughan Williams noted several songs in Herefordshire in July, 1908, including 'The Carnal and the Crane', no 43). 'No songs worth collecting': there is a certain *hauteur* here, but in connection with the material, not the informants. Ursula Vaughan Williams sums up her husband's respect for his singers: 'among the many people he had met on collecting expeditions some of the singers had been toughs and, possibly, rogues as well, but had the sensitivity to cherish their music' (*ibid*, p.401). Without his work, in most cases not only their songs but their names would now be lost, except perhaps to a few relatives. His collection is their memorial.

Of course, he did quarry it over the years. Many songs were published in different volumes of the *Journal of the Folk Song Society* (1899–1931), and some in its various successors. Vaughan Williams used tunes, sometimes married rather incongruously with sacred texts, and also complete songs in *The English Hymnal* (1906) and *The Oxford Book of Carols* (1928, with Martin Shaw). There were several small collections, such as *Fifteen Folk Songs from the Eastern Counties* (1908), *Eight Traditional English Carols* (1919) and *Twelve Traditional Carols from Herefordshire* (1920, with Mrs E. M. Leather). In addition, Vaughan Williams used folk songs and tunes directly in operas such as *Hugh the Drover* (1924) and in many orchestral and vocal compositions, from *In the Fen Country* (1904) to *Folk Songs of the Four Seasons*

(1949). Elsie Payne lists thirty-eight of his compositions 'which use or quote directly from folk song', both from his own collections and elsewhere (pp.105–6: article, 'Vaughan Williams and Folk Song' in *The Music Review*, 1954, pp.103–126). She also analyses the profound indirect effect on his music which folk song had.

More songs appeared posthumously, in *The Penguin Book of English Folk Songs* (1959, edited by R. Vaughan Williams and A. L. Lloyd), *A Yacre of Land* (1961, edited by U. Vaughan Williams and I. Holst), and in some of my own anthologies, notably *Everyman's Book of English Country Songs* (1979). At the same time, many of Vaughan Williams's earlier arrangements and volumes of folk song are now out of print, and in addition the bulk of his collection has remained in manuscript. Eighty years after the collection was begun, and twenty-five years after Vaughan Williams's death, it seemed a good idea to gather a representative selection from his collection into one volume. One hundred and twenty-one songs out of the total of 810 have been included, of which 70 are hitherto unpublished. They have been grouped under counties, eighteen in number. As Vaughan Williams wrote in his introduction to *Folk Songs from the Eastern Counties* (1908): 'It is not to be supposed that they [the songs] are the exclusive property of the counties to which they are credited; all that is claimed for them is that they were certainly sung in those counties'. The arrangement has the additional advantage that each singer's songs can be gathered together, which in turn allows his or her repertoire, or at least that part of it noted by Vaughan Williams (and, where appropriate, by any other collectors) to be considered. To this end, the notes on sources give the number of songs collected from each singer by Vaughan Williams, and lists the details of any published. Of Vaughan Williams's 248 singers, 166 were men, 30 women and 52 unspecified. Seventy-four singers are included here, of whom 60 are men, ten women and four unspecified.

I have tried to make a representative selection from the collection, including certain well-known songs, such as 'Bushes and Briars' (no 16), 'The Captain's Apprentice' (no 53) and 'The Blacksmith' (no 48), which are inseparably linked with Vaughan Williams, and also some rarities. These include 'Elwina of Waterloo' (no 28), 'The Drowsy Sleeper' (no 49), 'Edward Jorgen' (no 58), 'Bonny Robin' (no 73), 'The Ranter Parson' (no 89), 'Hurricane Wind' (no 100), 'The Witty Lass of London' (no 103), 'Duke William' (no 111), 'The Convict's Lamentation' (no 114) and 'The Cheshire Gate' (no 115). In between lies the stock-in-trade of English country singers during the early years of this century. There are a few items of Scots origin, such as 'Bonnie Susie Cleland' (no

3), 'Long Lankin' (no 29) and 'John Raeburn' (no 62), one each from America ('The *Cumberland*'s Crew, no 60) and Australia (no 114), and several from Ireland: 'The Pride of Kildare' (no 1), 'Brennan on the Moor' (no 15), 'The Lads of Kilkenny' (no 88) and 'The Young Servant Man' (no 104). Most, however, seem unequivocally English, though many of them can also be found in North America. Songs for which Vaughan Williams obtained words have been chosen as far as possible, though some deficiencies in texts have been made up from street ballads.

In content, there is a marked leaning towards the sea, which is partly explained by the singers' predilection for nautical themes, partly no doubt by the fact that ten of the eighteen counties represented are maritime. Another major preoccupation (not necessarily divorced from the sea) is love and marriage, followed by war, work, crime, sport and adventure.

The question arises as to whether this selection from a selective

The heading of a black-letter ballad printed in about 1670.
(See 'Cupid the Ploughboy', no 106).
Courtesy of the Bodleian Library, Oxford

[xxi]

collection can have any claim to being representative of English country song. Because of Vaughan Williams's preoccupation with fine tunes, there is undoubtedly a higher proportion of modal melodies than would have been the case in a random sample. Conversely, there are few if any of the music hall songs which would undoubtedly have been in the repertoires of many of the singers. Some favourite songs, such as 'The Seeds of Love', 'Jones' Ale', 'Maria Marten' and 'Van Diemen's Land', although they are in Vaughan Williams's collection, have been omitted here since his versions have been published very recently.

Despite these qualifications I believe the selection to be wide-ranging and representative. The subject matter is diverse. There are fourteen Child ballads, some home-made songs, and many pieces with close links with broadsides, some dating from the seventeenth century, some of recent origin. The mood ranges from bawdy to idyllic, from farcical to tragic. There are introspective lyrics and roaring tavern songs, jog-trot tunes and soaring airs.

Vaughan Williams considered these fine melodies to be part of a 'precious heritage', and he believed 'some rare old ballad or an exquisitely beautiful melody worthy, within its smaller compass, of a place beside the finest compositions of the greatest composers' (*Journal*, vol. II, preface to part 8). Vaughan Williams is a composer of the first rank who owes a good deal to folk song, but folk song owes a great deal to him. As we have seen, it is possible from our viewpoint seventy years on to have reservations about his methods of collecting, but the predominant feeling should be immense gratitude that he should have made his collection at all, and beyond that to have spent so much time in annotating, arranging and promoting folk song. We are deeply indebted to him.

BERKSHIRE

1   The Pride of Kildare

Like many other songs of Irish origin, this was widely sung in England, no doubt helped by its frequent appearances on nineteenth-century street ballads. An aged Derbyshire woman interviewed in 1906 remembered seeing a copy nailed to the loom, and a weaver singing as she wove (S. O. Addy, 'Little Hucklow: its customs and houses', in *Derbyshire Archaeological Journal*, 1906, p.20). This version, however, was sung by the son of the landlady at *The Chequers Inn*, Cookham Dean, Berkshire.

When— first from sea I land-ed I had a ro-ving mind. Un-daunt-ed I ram-bled, my true love to find. There I be-held pret-ty Su-san with cheeks like the rose, And her bo-som more fair than the li-ly that grows.

2 Her keen eyes did glitter like bright stars by night,
   And the robes she was wearing were costly and white;
   Her bare neck was shaded with her long raven hair,
   And they called her pretty Susan, the pride of Kildare.

3 Long time her I courted, till I wasted my store,
   When her love turned to hatred because I was poor.
   She said: 'I love another, whose portion I'll share,
   So begone from pretty Susan, the pride of Kildare'.

4 Oh, my heart ached next morning as lonely I did stray,
   I espied pretty Susan with a young lord so gay;
   And as I passed by them with my heart full of care,
   I sighed for pretty Susan, the pride of Kildare.

5 Once more on the ocean I resolved for to go,
   And was bound to the east with my heart full of woe,
   Where I beheld ladies in jewels so rare,
   But none like pretty Susan, the pride of Kildare.

6 Sometimes I am jovial, sometimes I am sad,
   Since my love she is courted by some other lad;
   But since we are at a distance, no more I'll despair.
   So my blessing to Susan, the pride of Kildare.

BUCKINGHAMSHIRE

2   I Had One Man

In its better-known guise as 'One Man Went to Mow', this was, according to Robert Graves, the most popular marching song of the Great War. Originally, it was intended to lighten labour in the fields, though mowing meadows is so widely used as a sexual metaphor that it is hard to avoid hearing erotic overtones. Vaughan Williams took down only the first verse, but a similar version from Nova Scotia continued up to 34 men, and another from Oxfordshire to 100.

I had one man, I had two men To mow down my mea-dow. I had three men, I had four men To car-ry my hay a-way. My four men, my three men, My two men, my one man, And all no more. *CHORUS* To mow my hay, To carry it a-way, And all for jol-ly good fun.

2 I had five men, I had six men
  To mow down my meadow.
  I had seven men, I had eight men
  To carry my hay away.
  My eight men, my seven men,
  My six men, my five men,
  And all no more.

3 I had nine men, I had ten men
   To mow down my meadow.
   I had eleven men, I had twelve men
   To carry my hay away.
   My twelve men, my eleven men,
   My ten men, my nine men,
   And all no more.

And so on, *ad lib.*

3   Bonnie Susie Cleland

Like 'I Had One Man', this comes from a tailor, Mr Wetherill, who
learned his songs in public houses. It is the only version – albeit
fragmentary – of 'Bonnie Susie Cleland' which has turned up in
England. The scrap of text has been completed from Motherwell's
Minstrelsy Ancient and Modern (1827). There was once a notion,
widespread through Europe, that 'incontinence' (Professor Child's
genteel term for fornication) on the part of unmarried women attracted
in Scotland the penalty of burning to death. Aside from the possibility
that this might well have decimated, at least, the unmarried female
population, it was simply not true. The penalties for 'incontinence' for
both sexes, at least between 1563 and 1784, were, for a first offence, a
fine and two hours in the pillory; for a second, a bigger fine, pillory and
having the head shaven; for a third, a stiffer fine still, a triple ducking
and perpetual banishment. In all conscience, this was bad enough, but
writers of romances, like Ariosto in *Orlando Furioso*, and also singers,
continued to believe the worst.

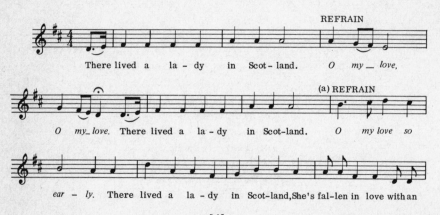

[4]

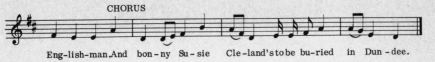

Eng-lish-man.And bon-ny Su-sie Cle-land's to be bu-ried in Dun-dee.

Var.(a)

2 The father unto the daughter came,
  Saying, 'Will you forsake that Englishman?

3 'If you will not that Englishman forsake,
  O I will burn you at the stake'.

4 'I will not that Englishman forsake,
  Though you should burn me at a stake.

5 'O where will I get a pretty little boy
  Who will carry tidings to my joy?'

6 'Here am I, a pretty little boy
  Who will carry tidings to thy joy'.

7 'Give to him this right-hand glove.
  Tell him to find another love.

8 'Give to him this little penknife.
  Tell him to get another wife.

9 'Give to him this gay gold ring.
  Tell him I'm going to my burning.'

10 Her father dragged her to a stake;
   Her mother then a fire did make.

CAMBRIDGESHIRE

4   **May Song**

Bringing home greenery on the early morning of May Day was a joyous pastime for young men and women up to Elizabethan times, when the custom started to come under attack on grounds of paganism and immorality. This May carol, 'sung from time immemorial in the villages of Fowlmere and Thriplow' (according to the Rev C. H. E. White, who took down a version in 1898), is somewhat gloomy, largely because of verses dealing with the passion of Christ, which have been absorbed from elsewhere. Vaughan Williams used it in several publications and also in his opera, *Hugh the Drover* (1924), of which Ursula Vaughan Williams writes: 'The May song, starting off stage and coming nearer, recalls a story told him by 'Hoppy' Flack, a singer at Fowlmere, near Cambridge, from whom he collected it. When Hoppy was young he and his friends would go out each May eve, singing all through the short darkness and being given drinks at each house they visited. As time went on the singers became less enthusiastic, and finally only he and another elderly man kept up the custom. Hoppy's head was by then less good than it might have been, or, there being only two of them, they drank more at each call. On their way he slipped and fell into a ditch, and his friend failed to pull him out of it. Not wishing to lose the money they were to be given as well as refreshment, the friend went on. Hoppy lay there listening to the May song, now near, now further away, as the dawn was breaking and his friend went singing from cottage to cottage till it was day' (*R.V.W. A Biography of Ralph Vaughan Williams*, 1964, p.401). That was the true spirit of May Day.

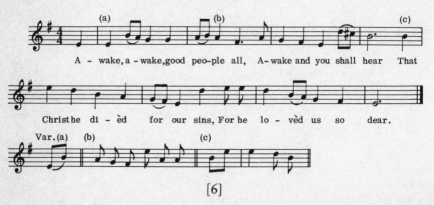

A - wake, a - wake, good peo-ple all, A-wake and you shall hear That

Christ he di - èd for our sins, For he lo - vèd us so dear.

Var. (a)   (b)   (c)

2 So dearly, so dearly has Christ lovèd us,
   And he for our sins was slain.
   Christ bids us leave off our wickedness
   And return to the Lord again.

3 The early cock so early crows,
   He is passing the night away;
   For the trumpet shall sound and the dead shall be raised,
   Lord, at the great judgement day.

4 A branch of May I have brought to you,
   And at your door it stands;
   It is but a sprout, it's well budded out,
   By the work of our Lord's hands.

5 Now my song, that is done and I must be gone,
   No longer can I stay.
   God bless you all, both great and small,
   And I wish you a joyful May.

5   Lord Ellenwater

The Derwentwater family had estates in Cumberland and Northumberland. The family seat, originally on an island in Derwentwater (hence the name) was abandoned in the seventeenth century in favour of Dilston Hall, near Corbridge. James Ratcliffe, the third Lord Derwentwater, and subject of the ballad, seems to have been genuinely loved by his family, servants and tenants. When he was beheaded in 1716, for his involvement in the abortive Jacobite rising of the previous year, he was widely mourned. A tune, 'Derwentwater's Farewell', can still be heard in the north-east, and versions of the ballad, albeit with some confusion over details, circulated orally for some two hundred years. The multiplicity of ill omens in the first three verses leaves the tragic outcome in no doubt.

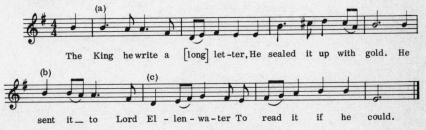

The King he write a [long] let-ter, He sealed it up with gold. He sent it _ to Lord El-len-wa-ter To read it if he could.

[7]

2 The first few lines that he did read
  It caused him for to smile;
  And the next few words that he did read
  Made the tears trickle down from his eyes.

3 'O saddle me my milk-white steed,
  Get it ready with all speed';
  And the ring from his little finger did burst,
  And his nose had begun to bleed.

4 He was going along the high-road,
  His horse it stumbled at a stone.
  'It's a token', says Lord Ellenwater,
  'That I never shall return'.

5 Now when he came to fair London
  Among the high quality,
  There were lords and dukes and all sorts of gentlemen,
  But a traitor they called him all.

6 'No traitor', cries Lord Ellenwater,
  'No traitor you never knew me,
  For I'm keeping of five thousand brave men
  To fight in my own country'.

7 Then up did step a brave old man
  With a drawn sword in his hand:
  'Make your will, make your will, Lord Ellenwater,
  For your life is at my command'.

8 'If my life is at your command
  One thing I will freely give:
  The green velvet coat that I have got on
  You shall have it for your fee.

9 'And here's one thing more that I have to ask
  Or shameful [shall] I die,
  O the lords and the dukes in fair London town
  Shall be kind to my fair lady'.

6 The Keeper

Those who were at school between the 1920s and the 1950s will almost certainly remember singing 'The Keeper' in a Warwickshire version collected by Cecil Sharp, and lightly but effectively bowdlerised by him (though we did not know this at the time) to make it into a jolly hunting song instead of a litany of sexual pursuit. The earliest known version is a black-letter ballad of fifteen verses, written by one Joseph Martin, and published in the mid-1680s under the title of 'The Huntsman's Delight; or The Forester's Pleasure'. In the eighteenth century a slightly less elaborate version was issued, this time in white-letter, with only six verses, and entitled 'The Frolicksome Keeper. A New Song'. Unlike its predecessor, it has the dialogue chorus which is common to versions which have turned up in oral tradition during this century.

2 The first doe he shot at he missed,
   The second doe he shot he kissed,
   The third she ran right over the heath ...

3 The fourth doe she leaped over the brook,
   The keeper catched her fast with his hook,
   And what he did there you may go and look ...

4 The fifth doe she ran over the plain,
   The keeper fetched her back again,
   And tickled her in a merry, merry vein ...

5 The sixth doe she leaped over the stile,
   The keeper catched her fast by the heel,
   And there he did both tickle and feel ...

6 The seventh doe she did prove with fawn,
   And to the keeper she made great moan,
   A-wishing he'd but let her alone ...

7   The Lousy Tailor

The popular tradition gave short shrift to tailors, because of their alleged
pusillanimity and their participation in a trade regarded as unmasculine.
It seems that Vaughan Williams was so horrified by the words of this
song that he did not note any of them, save the vocables of the refrains.
He used the sprightly Dorian tune for another text, but it is here re-
united with what I take to be a version of the original words, a broadside
entitled 'The Butcher and the Tailor's Wife'.

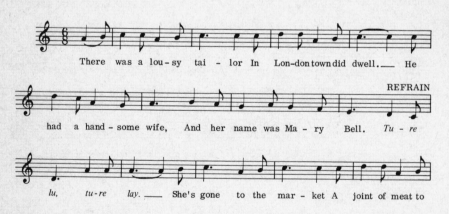

There was a lou-sy tai-lor In Lon-don town did dwell.__ He
had a hand-some wife, And her name was Ma-ry Bell. *Tu-re*
*lu, tu-re lay.*__ She's gone to the mar-ket A joint of meat to

[10]

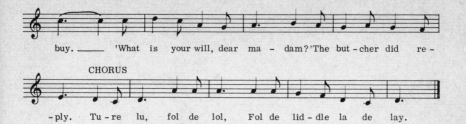

buy. _____ 'What is your will, dear ma - dam?' The but - cher did re -

CHORUS

-ply. Tu - re lu, fol de lol, Fol de lid - dle la de lay.

2 This joint was straight cut down,
  Refuse it she did not;
  Straightway she fetched it home
  And she put in the pot.
  The tailor he came home
  And she told him what she had,
  Then the tailor leaped for joy
  And his heart was very glad.

3 'Dear husband, O, dear husband,
  I'll tell you how it must be:
  Tomorrow night the butcher
  He is to lie with me;
  Take your broad sword in your hand
  And under the bed go,
  The first man that enters then,
  Be sure to run him through'.

4 'I never handled sword or gun,
  My dear, my loving wife.
  The butchers they are bloody dogs,
  I'm afraid he'll have my life'.
  'Do not you be faint-hearted,
  But with courage stout and bold,
  And if the butcher you o'ercome
  You'll wear a chain of gold'.

5 The butcher, thinking it was time
  To see the tailor's wife,
  And fearing they should form a plot,
  Or trick to take his life,
  Got a brace of pistols loaded
  With powder and with ball:
  'The man that molests me now,
  By Jove, I'll make him fall'.

[11]

6 When the butcher he came by
  She took him by the hand,
  And led him to her bed-chamber:
  'Sir, I'm at your command'.
  He pulled out his brace of pistols
  And laid them on the bed.
  The tailor was struck with fear;
  He lay as if quite dead.

7 As the butcher took off his clothes
  To get into the bed,
  How he was struck when he did spy
  One of the tailor's legs.
  'Is this your husband's dog?', he says;
  'I'll shoot him for the fright'.
  'O, spare my life', the tailor cries,
  'And you shall have my wife'.

8   The Nine Joys of Mary

Most ancient songs continuing to be sung have been abbreviated with the passage of time. However, this one started as five joys in the fourteenth century and became seven in the fifteenth. (These were the Annunciation, Visitation, Nativity, Adoration of the Magi, Presentation in the Temple, Christ found by his mother, the Assumption and Coronation of the Virgin). Richard Hill (for whom, see no 12) included the 'seven' version in his commonplace book, which was compiled in about 1500. In the eighteenth and nineteenth centuries the joys gradually extended to a maximum of twelve, with all sorts of fanciful variations, including to write without a pen (number ten), and some particularly atrocious rhymes for number twelve: to ring the heavenly bells, or to have the keys of hell.

The first good joy that Ma-ry had it was the joy of one, To see her own son Je - sus to suck at the breast-

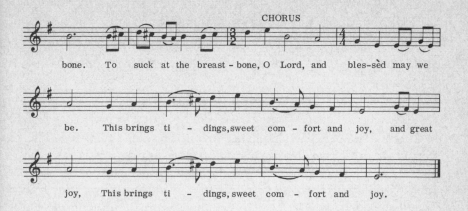

CHORUS

bone. To suck at the breast - bone, O Lord, and bles-sèd may we

be. This brings ti - dings, sweet com - fort and joy, and great

joy, This brings ti - dings, sweet com - fort and joy.

2 The next ... two ... to read the Bible through.

3 The next ... three ... to make the blind to see.

4 The next ... four ... to say the Bible o'er.

5 The next ... five ... to raise the dead alive.

6 The next ... six ... to bear the crucifix.

7 The next ... seven ... to eat the bread of Heaven.

8 The next ... eight ... to make the crooked straight.

9 The next ... nine ... to turn water into wine.

CUMBERLAND

9   **Blackwell Merry Night**

In August 1906, Vaughan Williams took down seven tunes from a Mr Carruthers at Carlisle, noting that 'all the words are from Anderson's book'. The singer was probably John Carruthers of Wigton. 'Anderson's book' is *Cumberland Ballads*, a collection of dialect songs written to traditional tunes, which earned its author, Robert Anderson (1770–1833), the title of the Cumbrian Burns. The book went through many editions and the songs became firm favourites, some circulating orally for a hundred years and more. Poor Anderson died of drink and poverty, but his songs are still full of life. 'Blackwell Merry Night' ('Blackell Murry Neet' in the original – I have softened the dialect) features a New Year celebration at a village which is now part of Carlisle. Dancing played a big part, as the poet Keats found on a visit to Cumberland in 1818, when he wrote: 'They kickit and jumpit with mettle extraordinary, and whiskit and friskit, and toed it and goe'd it, and twirl'd it and whirl'd it and stamped it, and sweated it, tattooing the floor like mad'.

Aye, lad, such a merry night we've had at Blackwell, The sound of the fid-dle still rings in my ear. All well clipped and heeled were the lads and the las-ses, And ma-ny a live-ly young las-sie was there. The bet-ter sort they sat snug in the par-lour; In the pan-try the sweet-hearts they

[14]

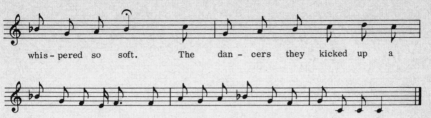

whis-pered so soft. The dan-cers they kicked up a

dust in the kit-chen; At lan-ter the card-play-ers sat in the loft.

2 The clogger from Dawston's a famous top hero,
   And beats all the player-folk twenty to one.
   He stamped with his foot and shouted and roystered,
   Till the sweat it ran off his very chin end.
   Then he held up a hand like the spout of a tea-pot,
   And danced 'Cross the Buckle' and 'Leather to Patch';
   When they cried 'Bonny Bell' he leapt up to the ceiling,
   And kept snapping his thumbs for a bit of a fratch.

3 The Heverby lads were well used to deep drinking;
   At cocking the Dawstoners never were beat.
   The Buckabank chaps were right famous at courting;
   Their kisses just sound like the latch of a gate.
   The lasses of Blackwell are so many angels,
   The Cummersdale beauties all glory in fun.
   God help the poor fellow that squints at them dancing:
   He'll steal away heartless as sure as a gun.

4 The bacca was strong and the ale it was lively,
   And many a one emptied a quart like a churn.
   Daft Fred in the nook like a half-roasted devil
   Told smutty stories and made them all grin.
   Then one sang 'Tom Linton', another 'Dick Walters';
   The farmers bragged of their fillies and foals,
   With jibing and joking and shaking and laughing,
   Till some thought it time to set off to the coals.

5 But hold, I forgot. When the clock struck eleven
   The platter was brought in with white bread and brown;
   The knife it was sharp, the great cheese was a topper,
   And lumps big as lapstones our lads gobbled down.
   The trim, jolly landlady cried: 'Eat and welcome.
   In God's name, step forward; do not be shy'.
   Our guts were well filled, we paid up for blind Jenny,
   And next paid the shot on a great pewter plate.

[15]

6 Now full to the throttle, with headaches and heart-aches,
   Some crept to the clock-case instead of the door;
   Then sleeping and snoring took place of their roaring,
   And one atop another they laid on the floor.
   The last of December, long, long we'll remember,
   At five in the morn, eighteen hundred and three.
   Here's health and success to the brave Johnny Dawston,
   And many such meetings may we live to see.

clipped and heeled: properly dressed
  (as a cock prepared for a fight)
lanter: card game
clogger: clog-maker
cocking: cock-fighting
fratch: quarrel
heartless: having lost his heart to one
  of the girls
nook: ingle nook
'Tom Linton', 'Dick Walters': both by
  Anderson

lapstones: 'A stone that shoemakers
  lay in their laps to beat their leather
  aprons' (O.E.D).
shot: reckoning
eighteen hundred and three: the
  original has 'and twee' (and two),
  but 'three' has been used for the
  sake of the rhyme

10   Geordie Gill

Robert Anderson wrote with tenderness, affection and humour about
love and courtship. This song was written to the tune of 'Andro wi' his
Cutty Gun' in 1804. Geordie Gill seems to have been well known at the
time as a local heart-throb, and he is mentioned in at least one other
song by Anderson, 'Rob Lowrie'. There, a woman bewails at some
length the loss of her sweetheart, but at the drop of a hat turns to
Geordie Gill: 'But whee's this comes whuslin', sae sweet, owre the hill?/
He brings me a pwosey – It's e'en Gwordie Gill./He's lish, an' he's
canny, wi' reed curly hair –/The deil tek Rob Lowrie. I'll heed him nae
mair'.

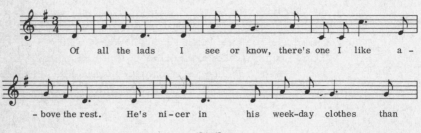

Of all the lads I see or know, there's one I like a-
- bove the rest. He's ni-cer in his week-day clothes than

[16]

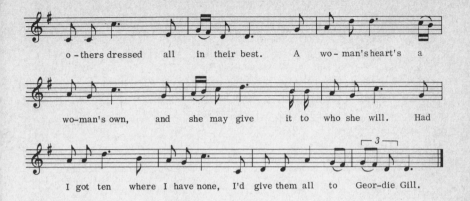

o - thers dressed all in their best. A wo - man's heart's a

wo-man's own, and she may give it to who she will. Had

I got ten where I have none, I'd give them all to Geor-die Gill.

2 Who was it stole our landlord's fruit for me when bairns we went to school?
Who was it dared go mid-thigh deep to get my coat out of the pool?
And when the filly flung me off, and long and long I laid so ill,
Who watched o'er me both night and day, and wished me well? It was
    Geordie Gill.

3 Oft mounted on his long-tailed nag, with fine new boots up to his knee,
The laird's daft son 'lights in the yard, and bows and scrapes to worry me.
Though father, mother, uncle, too, to wed this booby tease me still,
For all I hear of his land and brass, I still steal out to Geordie Gill.

4 From Carlisle cousin Fanny came and brought her white-faced sweetheart
    down,
With shirt-neck stuck above his lugs, a poor thin fellow from the town.
He minced and talked and skipped and walked, but tired going up the hill,
And looked as pale as any corpse, compared to rosy Geordie Gill.

5 My Geordie's whistle well I know long ere we meet the darkest night,
And when he lilts and sings 'Skewball', no playhouse music's half so sweet.
A woman's heart's a woman's own, and she may give it to who she will;
I had one once, now I have none, for it belongs to Geordie Gill.

'Skewball': song about a racehorse of this name

11   King Roger

Here Anderson uses with great skill the innocent eye of a child in a
variation on the ancient theme of the world turned upside down. The
tune originally intended was 'Hallow Fair', but the singer here used
'Sally Gray', which was also known to Anderson.

[17]

'Twas but t'other night af-ter dark-'ning, we sat o'er a bla-zing turf fire; Our lass she was stir-ring a cow-drink, our Bet-ty milked cows in the byre. 'Aye, fa-ther', cried out lit-tle Ro-ger, 'I wish I were nob-but a king'. 'Why, what would you do', says I, 'Ro-ger, sup-pose you could take your full swing?'———

2 'First, you should be lord judge and bishop; my mother should have a gold crutch.
I'd build for the poor folk fine houses and give them – aye, ever so much.
Our Betty should wed Charley Miggins and wear her print dress every day;
Such dancing we'd have in the cock-loft; Bill Adams the fiddle should play.

3 'A posset I'd have for my breakfast, and sup with a bright silver spoon;
For dinner I'd have a fat crowdy, and strong tea at mid-afternoon.
I'd wear nice white cotton stockings, and new gambaleery clean shoes,
With neat, lively, black fustian breeches and every fine thing I could choose.

4 'I'd have many thousands of shipping to sail the wide world all about.
I'd say to our soldiers: "Go over the seas, and kill the French dogs out and out".
On our long-tailed nag I'd be mounted, my footmen in silver and green,
And when I'd seen all foreign countries I'd make Aggy Glaister my queen.

5 'Our meadow should be a great orchard and grow nought at all but big plums.

[18]

A school house we'd build. As for master, we'd e'en hang him up by the
  thumbs.
Joss Feddon should be my head huntsman; we'd keep seven couple of dogs,
And kill all the hares in the kingdom: my mother should wear well-greased
  clogs.

6 'Then Christmas should last, aye for ever, and Sundays we'd have twice a
     week;
   The moon should show light all the winter; our cat and our colly should
     speak.
   The poor folk should live without working, and feed on plum-pudding and
     beef.
   Then all would be happy, for certain, there neither could be rogue or thief'.

7 Now thus run on little King Roger, but soon all his happiness fled:
   A spark from the fire burnt his knuckle, and off he crept crying to bed.
   Thus fares it with both young and old folk, from king to the beggar we see,
   Just cross us in the midst of our greatness, and poor wretched creatures are
     we.

cock-loft: loft over the barn
posset: hot milk curdled with ale or
  wine (considered a delicacy)
crowdy: gruel

gambaleery: very shiny leather
well-greased clogs: with the grease
  coming from the hares

12   Down in Yon Forest

During the early part of the sixteenth century, a London grocer called Richard Hill compiled a commonplace book. One of the items, the 'Corpus Christi Carol', takes its name from the inscription on a stone by the bed of a wounded knight who is watched over by a weeping 'may' (maiden). Numerous attempts have been made to explain the significance of this mysterious carol by referring to the Grail legends or to the passion of Christ. An ingenious theory is that it was a cryptic expression of sympathy for Queen Catherine at the time (1533) when she was displaced by Anne Boleyn, and also of concern at Henry VIII's treatment of the church. This may seem far-fetched but it is convincingly argued by R. L. Greene ('The Meaning of the Corpus Christi Carol', in *Medium Aevum*, XXIX, 1960, pp.10–21), who adds that his thesis 'does not reduce, but rather enhances, the richness of a poem which has some right to be called the most beautiful of all the English carols'. The first tune ever to be collected for it was sung to Vaughan Williams by a Castleton man, Mr J. Hall, who supplied a written copy of his version of the words.

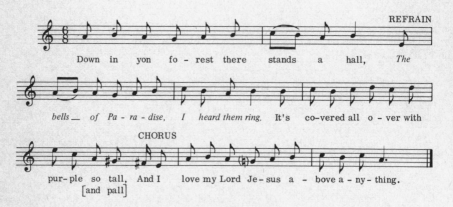

Down in yon fo - rest there stands a hall, *The* bells _ of Pa - ra - dise, *I* heard them ring. It's co - vered all o - ver with purple so tall, And I love my Lord Je - sus a - bove a - ny - thing.
[and pall]

2 In that hall there stands a bed,
  It's covered all over with scarlet so red.

3 In that bed there lies a knight,
  Whose wounds do bleed by day and night.

4 At the bedside there lies a stone,
   Which the sweet Virgin Mary knelt upon.

5 Under that bed there runs a river, [flood]
   The one half runs water, the other runs blood.

6 At the foot of the bed there grows a thorn,
   Which ever bore blossom since he was born.

7 Over that bed the moon shines bright,
   Denoting our saviour was born on this night.

DURHAM

13   The Green Bed

A sailor returning from sea pleads poverty in order to test the true feelings towards him of a public house landlady and her daughter. They reject him, not even offering the 'green bed' – a temporary bed made up when others were full, so called because of the practice of stuffing the mattress with greenery. They change their tune when Sailor John reveals his true riches, but he takes revenge by rejecting them in his turn. The song was often printed on street ballads in the nineteenth century, and was widely sung on both sides of the Atlantic.

A sailor of old England has lately come on shore, With his ragged apparel like one that is so poor. He went into an ale-house where he used for to lodge: 'You're welcome, dear John; I am glad you're home from sea.'

2 'Last night my daughter, Polly, lay dreaming of thee'.
'And your daughter, Polly, I should wish for to see.
We've had sad misfortune, our ship and cargo lost;
All on the wide ocean my fortune has been tossed'.

[22]

3 'If that's been your misfortune, John, I'll have no more to you,
   Nor never wish to trust you with one pot or two'.
   Young John being drowsy he hung down his head,
   He called for a candle to light him to bed.

4 'My beds are all engaged, John, and have been all the week,
   And so, young John, fresh lodgings you must go and seek'.
   'If to a fresh lodging you force me to go,
   What is it I owe to you and down I will pay'.

5 'There is five and forty shillings, John, thou hast owed me of old',
   And out of his pocket he pulled handfuls of gold.
   At the sight of the gold the landlady knew not what to think.
   She said, 'John, sit down, while I go and fetch some drink.

6 'If you was in earnest, John, I own I was in jest,
   But above all men in this world, young John I love best'.
   Young Polly hearing this down the stairs she did run,
   And many a pleasant look oh she looked upon John.

7 She huddled him, she cuddled him, she callèd him her dear:
   'The green bed is empty, you and I shall sleep there'.
   'Before I'd sleep all in your bed I'd sleep all out of door.
   Before I'd marry your daughter I'd marry a common whore'.

8 Come all you jolly sailors that plough the watery main,
   That earnès your money by cold, wet and the rain,
   Be careful of your money, boys, and lap it up in store,
   [For when your money's gone] they'll kick you out of door.

five and forty shillings: £2.25   *lap:* wrap

14   Franklin's Crew

Sir John Franklin set off in 1845 to attempt to find a north-west passage
round North America, then disappeared. His two ships were last seen to
the north of Baffin Bay. In 1850 Sir John Ross set out to find the lost
expedition, but returned unsuccessful. Further attempts, vigorously
supported by Lady Jane Franklin, fared no better until 1859, when
diaries were found in a cairn and solved the mystery. Franklin's ships
had been trapped in the ice off King William Island for eighteen months,
when the explorer had died (June, 1847). The crews had then set out to
trek to safety, but every man had perished. The enigma and Lady

Franklin's desperate search inspired several street ballads, one of which entered oral tradition on both sides of the Atlantic, usually to a tune normally associated with execution songs (see no 58). It was sung not merely by landsmen but by sailors themselves, as we know from Joseph Faulkner's *Eighteen Months on a Greenland Whaler*, where it appears as 'The Sailor's Dream' (New York, 1878, pp.73–4).

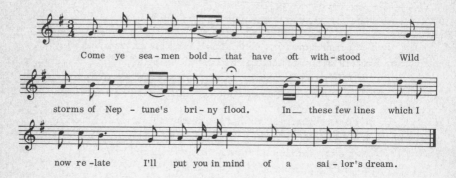

Come ye sea-men bold — that have oft with-stood Wild storms of Nep - tune's bri-ny flood. In — these few lines which I now re -late I'll put you in mind of a sai - lor's dream.

2 As homeward bound one night on the deep,
   Slung in my hammock I fell fast asleep.
   I dreamed a dream which I thought was true,
   Concerning Franklin and his brave crew.

3 I thought as we neared to the Humber shore
   I heard a female that did deplore;
   She wept aloud, and seemed to say:
   'Alas, my Franklin is long away.

4 'Long time it is since two ships of fame
   Did bear my husband across the main,
   With a hundred seamen with courage stout
   To find a north western passage out.

5 'With a hundred seamen with hearts so bold,
   I fear have perished with frost and cold.
   Alas', she cried, 'all my life I'll mourn,
   Since Franklin seems never to return.

6 'There's Captain Austen of Scarborough Town,
   Brave Granville and Penny, of much renown,
   With Captain Ross, and so many more
   Have long been searching the Arctic shore.

7 'They sailèd east and they sailèd west,
   Round Greenland's coast they knew the best;

In hardships drear they have vainly strove,
On mountains of ice their ships were drove.

8 'At Baffin's Bay, where the whale fish blows,
The fate of Franklin nobody knows;
Which causes many a wife to mourn
In grievous sorrow for their return.

9 'These sad forebodings they give me pain
For the long-lost Franklin across the main,
Likewise the fate of so many before
Who have left their homes to return no more'.

15   Brennan on the Moor

'This Brennan', wrote P. W. Joyce, 'was a noted highwayman, who, in
the eighteenth century, ran his career in the Kilworth mountains near
Fermoy in Cork, and in the neighbourhood' (*Old Irish Folk Music and
Songs*, 1909, p.186). Like all the best highwaymen, he robbed from the
rich and gave to the poor; as one broadside has it, 'A brace of loaded
pistols he carried night and day,/He never robbed a poor man upon the
King's highway;/But what he'd taken from the rich, like Turpin and
Black Bess,/He always did divide it with the widow in distress'. Brennan
was hanged in 1804, but his touching ballad continued to be sung for
more than a century afterwards, not only in Ireland, but also in England
and America. The version given here came from an unnamed inmate of
Barnard Castle Workhouse, with a tune more usually associated with
'The Tailor in the Tea Chest'.

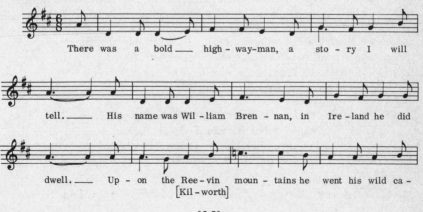

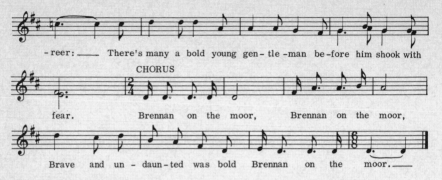

-reer: ——— There's many a bold young gen-tle-man be-fore him shook with

CHORUS

fear.   Brennan on the moor,   Brennan on the moor,

Brave   and un-daun-ted   was bold   Brennan   on   the   moor. ———

2 One night he robbed the packman, his name was Pedlar Brown.
   They travelled on together till the day began to dawn.
   The pedlar seeing his money gone, likewise his watch and chain,
   He at once encountered Brennan and robbed him back again.

3 When Brennan saw the pedlar as good a man as he,
   He took him on the king's highway, companion for to be.
   The pedlar thrust away his pack, without any more delay,
   And proved a right good comrade until his dying day.

4 One day upon the highway as William he went down
   He met the mayor of Cashel a mile outside the town;
   The mayor he knew his features, 'I think, young man', says he,
   'If your name is William Brennan you must come along with me'.

5 His wife went down to market then some provisions for to buy;
   When she saw William Brennan she began to weep and cry.
   He says: 'Lend me the tenpence'; and as poor William spoke
   She handed him the blunderbuss from underneath her cloak.

6 Then with his loaded blunderbuss, the truth I will unfold,
   He robbed the mayor of Cashel, he robbed him of his gold.
   One hundred pounds he did lay down for his apprehension there,
   So with his horse and saddle to the mountains did repair.

7 Then Brennan being an outlaw upon the mountains high,
   The cavalry and infantry to take him they did try.
   Brennan lost his fore-finger, taken off by a cannon ball,
   Then he and his comrade was taken after all.

8 Farewell unto my wife, and to my children three,
   Likewise my aged father, he may shed tears for me;
   And to my loving mother, who tore her hair and cried,
   Saying, 'I wish that William Brennan in the cradle he had died'.

tenpence: rebel term for a musket, from the price at which it was sold

ESSEX

16   Bushes and Briars

In the late autumn of 1903, after giving a lecture on folk song at Brentwood, Vaughan Williams was approached by two middle-aged ladies. They explained that their father, the Vicar of Ingrave, was about to give a tea-party for some old people in the village, who might conceivably know some songs. Vaughan Williams accepted an invitation to attend, met various singers, and returned the following day, 4 December, 1903, to note 26 songs. Up to that time, he wrote: 'I knew and loved the few English folk songs which were then available in printed collections, but I only believed in them vaguely, just as the layman believes in the facts of astronomy; my faith was not yet active.' When Vaughan Williams heard 'Bushes and Briars' he 'felt it was something he had known all his life'. It was the first folk song he noted, only three months after Cecil Sharp's first, 'The Seeds of Love'. The singer was a seventy-year-old labourer, Charles Pottipher, who, when asked about this and other of his songs, said: 'If you can get the words the Almighty will send you the tune.' Vaughan Williams took down the melody, commenting: 'It is impossible to reproduce the free rhythm and subtle portamento effects of this beautiful tune in ordinary notation.' He noted the words of the first verse only, later completing the text from a broadside issued by Fortey of Seven Dials.

Through bu-shes and through bri-ars I late-ly took my way, All for to hear the small birds sing, And the lambs to skip and play.

2 I overheard my own true love,
   Her voice it was so clear:
   'Long time I have been waiting
   For the coming of my dear'.

3 I drew myself unto a tree,
   A tree that did look green,
   Where the leaves shaded over us,
   We scarcely could be seen.

4 I sat myself down by my love
   Till she began to mourn:
   'I'm of this opinion
   That my heart is not my own.

5 'Sometimes I am uneasy
   And troubled in my mind;
   Sometimes I think I'll go to my love
   And tell to him my mind.

6 'And if I should go to my love,
   My love he will say "nay":
   I show to him my boldness,
   He'd ne'er love me again.

7 'I cannot think the reason
   Young women love young men,
   For they are so false-hearted,
   Young women to trepan.

8 'For they are so false-hearted,
   Young women to trepan,
   So the green grave shall see me,
   For I can't love that man'.

trepan: entrap

17   The Golden Glove

In his *Ancient Poems, Ballads and Songs of the Peasantry of England* (1846), J. H. Dixon wrote: 'This is a very popular ballad, and sung in every part of England. It is traditionally reported to be founded on an incident which occurred in the reign of Elizabeth.' The noble lady's *coup de foudre* for her social inferior would not have been out of place in a

Shakespearean plot; nor, for that matter, in a Victorian romantic novel. Her stratagem is altogether lacking in directness, however, for the late twentieth century, and the song is now very little heard. This version was sung in 1904 by Mrs Humphrys, who learned it from her grandmother, Ann Smyth (born at Blackmore, Essex, in 1794). Although the song travelled the country its location remained firmly anchored at Tamworth, in Staffordshire.

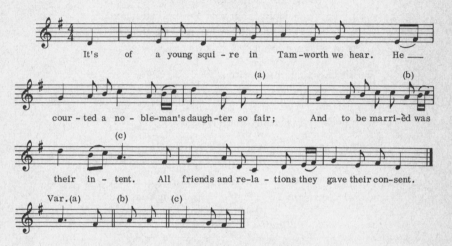

It's of a young squi - re in Tam-worth we hear. He —
(a)
cour - ted a no - ble-man's daugh -ter so fair; And to be marri-èd was
(b)
(c)
their in - tent. All friends and re-la - tions they gave their con-sent.
Var.(a) (b) (c)

2 The time was appointed for the wedding day,
A young farmer chosen to give her away;
As soon as the farmer the young lady did spy
He inflamèd her heart. 'O, my heart', she did cry.

3 She turned from the squire, but nothing she said;
Instead of being married she took to her bed.
The thought of the farmer soon run in her mind;
A way for to have him she quickly did find.

4 Coat, waistcoat and breeches she then did put on,
And a-hunting she went with her dog and her gun;
She hunted all round where the farmer did dwell,
Because in her heart she did love him full well.

5 She oftentimes fired but nothing she killed.
At length the young farmer came into the field,
And to discourse with him it was her intent;
With her dog and her gun to meet him she went.

6 'I thought you had been at the wedding', she cried,
'To wait on the squire and give him his bride'.

[29]

'No, sir', said the farmer, 'if the truth I may tell,
I'll not give her away, for I love her too well'.

7   'Suppose that the lady should grant you her love,
You know that the squire your rival will prove'.
'Why then', says the farmer, 'I'll take sword in hand;
By honour I'll gain her when she shall command'.

8   It pleased the lady to find him so bold;
She gave him a glove that was flowered with gold,
And told him she found it when coming along,
As she was a-hunting with her dog and her gun.

9   The lady went home with a heart full of love,
And gave out a notice that she'd lost a glove;
And said, 'Who has found it and brings it to me,
Whoever he is, he my husband shall be'.

10 The farmer was pleased when he heard of the news;
With heart full of joy to the lady he goes.
'Dear, honoured lady, I've picked up your glove,
And hope you'll be pleasèd to grant me your love'.

11 'It's already granted, I will be your bride;
I love the sweet breath of a farmer', she cried.
'I'll be mistress of my dairy, and milking my cow,
While my jolly brisk farmer is whistling at plough'.

12 And when she was married she told of her fun,
How she went a-hunting with her dog and her gun;
And said, 'Now I've got him so fast in my snare,
I'll enjoy him for ever, I vow and declare'.

young farmer chosen to give her away: the practice of the bride being given
away by her father is relatively recent.

18   The Cambric Shirt

Contests of wit and wisdom, in the shape of riddles, have determined
certain marriage partners, at least in literature, since the *Gesta
Romanorum*, a collection of tales compiled in the early fourteenth
century, and the source of the casket scene in *The Merchant of Venice*.
In one of the tales a king promised to marry a maiden if she could make
him a shirt out of a piece of linen three inches square. She said she

would, if he could supply a suitable implement. He sent her one (unspecified); she made the shirt; and they were wed. Something roughly analogous crops up in a black-letter broadside of about 1670, which has been attributed to James I of Scotland. In 'A proper new ballad entitled The Wind hath blown my Plaid away, or, A Discourse betwixt a young Woman and the Elphin Knight' a maiden fancies a knight as a husband, but he says she must first make him a shirt without cut or hem, shape it 'knife-and-sheerlesse' and sew it 'needle-threedlesse'. She ripostes by asking him to plough an acre of land with his hunting horn, sow it, build a cart of lime and stone and get Robin Redbreast to pull the harvest home. As if this were not enough, he must store it in a mousehole, thresh it in his shoe, winnow it in the palm of his hand, sack it in his glove and, finally, bring it over the sea dry. Then she will make him the shirt in the prescribed manner. Not surprisingly, he declines the bargain, and reveals that he already has a wife and seven children. About a century later a different form of the ballad became dominant. The action was reduced to the central debate between the two protagonists over the shirt and the acre of land. New refrains appeared: 'Parsley, sage, rosemary and thyme' and 'Once she (he) was a true lover of mine'. The tunes were invariably in triple time. The first appearance in print of 'The Cambric Shirt' was in *Gammer Gurton's Garland* (1784); later versions were sometimes called 'Scarborough Fair' or 'The Lover's Tasks'. Finally, in about the middle of the nineteenth century, a third variety (or degeneration) emerges, usually entitled 'An Acre of Land' (for which, see no 116). Like the previous song, the version of 'The Cambric Shirt' given here comes from Mrs Humphrys, who learned it from her father.

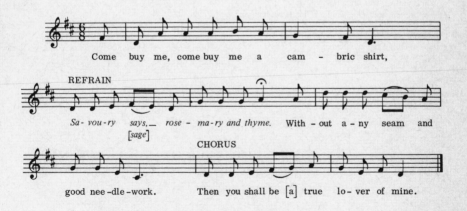

Come buy me, come buy me a cam - bric shirt,

REFRAIN
Sa - vou - ry says, — rose - ma - ry and thyme. With - out a - ny seam and
[sage]

CHORUS
good nee - dle - work. Then you shall be [a] true lo - ver of mine.

2 'Come wash it out in yonders well,
    Where the spring never dropt nor drop ever fell.

[31]

3 'Come hang it all out on yonder thorn
   That never has blew blossom since Adam was born'.

4 'And now you have asked me questions three,
   And now I will ask as many of thee.

5 'Come buy me, come buy me, an acre of land
   Between the sea water and the sea sand.

6 'Come plough it up with one ram's horn,
   And sow it all over with one peppercorn.

7 'Come harrow it all over with one bramble bush,
   And cut it all down with one royal rush.

8 'And make me a wagon with hair and lime,
   And cart it all home with six jenny wrens.

9 'Stack it all up in a mouse's hole,
   And thresh it all out with an old shoe sole.

10 'And fan it all up in an oyster shell,
   And stack it all up in a goose's quill.

11 'And then go to market my corn to sell,
   And bring home the money as I may a-tell.

12 'And when you've done and finished your work,
   And then come to me for your own cambric shirt'.

Savoury etc.: the Opies suggest that   *fan*: winnow
   this may have been an incantation.   *tell*: count

19   New Garden Fields

'New Spring Garden' was another name for the pleasure gardens at
Vauxhall in London, which were in existence from 1661 until 1859.
However, this sentimental song, with its references to goddesses and
Cupids, and its flowery phrases like 'earthly store' and 'bonds of love',
may merely refer to an imaginary Arcadia. For my money it must date
from the eighteenth century, though the earliest copies I have seen come
from the broadside presses of the early nineteenth, printed by Catnach,
Such (London), Russell (Birmingham) and Ford (Chesterfield). It seldom
appears in published collections of folk songs, though it was popular

with country singers like the Essex woodcutter of whom Vaughan Williams wrote: 'Mr Broomfield is well known as a singer and has been known to go on for hours when well primed.' Broomfield sang in what Vaughan Williams took to be 'the traditional manner, shutting his eyes tight and *speaking* the last line at the end of the song'.

Come all — you pret-ty fair maids, I —— pray you now at-
-tend Un - to these few lines I'm a - go - ing to
pen, Un - to these few lines I'm a - go - ing to
write. She— is — my whole stu - dy and my dreams all the night.

2 On the seventeenth of August, the eighth month of the year,
   Down the new garden fields where I just met my dear,
   She appeared like some goddess or some young divine,
   And come like a torment to torture my mind.

3 'It's I am no torment, young man', she did say,
   'I am pulling these flowers so fresh and so gay;
   I am pulling these flowers which nature does yield,
   And I take great delight in the new garden field'.

4 And I said, 'Lovely Nancy, dare I make so bold
   Your lily-white hand one minute to hold?
   It will give me more pleasure than all earthly store,
   So grant me this favour and I'll ask you no more'.

5 And she turned and said, 'Young man, I fear you must jest.
   If I thought you were earnest I'd think myself blest;
   But my father is coming there now', she did say,
   'So fare you well, young man, it's I must away'.

6 So now she's gone and left me all in the bonds of love,
   Kind Cupid, protect me, and you powers above;

[33]

Kind Cupid, protect me, and pray take my part,
For she's guilty of murder and quite broke my heart.

7 She turned and said, 'Young man, I pity your moan;
I'll leave you no longer to sigh alone.
I will go along with you to some foreign part:
You are the first young man that has won my heart.

8 'We'll go to church on Sunday and married we'll be,
We'll join hands in wedlock and sweet unity;
We'll join hands in wedlock and vow to be true:
To father and mother we will bid adieu'.

this favour: variant reading: 'thus far'

20   The Old Garden Gate

This is one of many fine lyrics expressing the searing pain of lost love. Vaughan Williams wrote that the tune was 'a good example of the extraordinary breadth and melodic sweep ... to be found in English folk song'.

2 To hear my true love sing, my boys,
To hear what she'd got for to say.
It's now very near three quarters of a year
Since you and I together did stay.

3 Come now my love and sit down by me,
   Where the leaves are springing green.
   It's now very near three quarters of a year
   Since you and I together have been.

4 I will not come and sit down by you,
   Nor [yet] no other young man.
   Since you have been courting another young girl
   Your heart is no longer mine.

where the leaves . . .: variant: 'Beneath this fine (?) lofty oak'

21   Robin Hood and the Pedlar

Ballads of Robin Hood are mentioned as early as 1363; manuscript
copies survive from less than a century later; and printed texts began
with Wynken de Worde, early in the sixteenth century. However, 'The
Bold Pedlar and Robin Hood', as Child calls it, seems to have emerged
for the first time in the eighteenth century, and to have been printed in
the nineteenth. Dixon, who mentions 'several common stall copies',
took down in the 1840s a version from the 'oral recitation', of 'an aged
female in Bermondsey' who told him that 'she had often heard her
grandfather sing it' (*op.cit.*, p.71). If the ballad came late, it stayed late,
and has been frequently collected in Britain and North America.
Vaughan Williams's singer was a bricklayer, Mr Bell, who 'was born in
London but learnt all his songs about thirty years ago [1876] from two
men at Brentford and Shenstone under whom he served – one was a
chimney sweep and had been round with a hawker's van'.

[35]

2 The first he met were some troublesome men;
   Two troublesome men there met he,
   And one it was bold Robin Hood,
   And the other it was little John so free.

3 'What have you in your pack?' said bold Robin Hood.
   'What have you in your pack, come tell to me,
   For before you move one step from us
   One half of your pack shall belong to me'.

4 'I've several suits of the gay rich silk,
   And silken gowns, one, two and three;
   And there is not a man in fair Nottingham
   That can take one half of this pack from me'.

5 Then little John he drew out his sword;
   The pedlar by his pack did stand.
   They heaved about till they both did sweat,
   And he cried, 'Pedlar, pedlar, pray hold your hand'.

6 Then bold Robin Hood was a-standing by
   To see them fight most heartily.
   Says he, 'I can find a man of smaller scale
   That will whop the pedlar and likewise thee'.

7 Then Robin Hood he drew out his sword;
   The pedlar by his pack did stand.
   They heaved about till the blood did run,
   And he cried, 'Pedlar, pray hold your hand.

8 'What is your name?' said bold Robin Hood.
   'What is your name, come tell to me'.
   'My name to you I will never tell
   Till both of your names you have told to me'.

9 'My name it is bold Robin Hood
   And the other is little John so free'.
   'And now it lies in my goodwill
   Whether I tell you my name or nay.

10 'But I'm Gamble Goff from the merry green woods,
   I'm Gamble Goff from over the seas.
   For killing a man in my father's land
   From my native country was forced to flee'.

11 'If you are Gamble Goff from the merry green woods,
   And Gamble Goff from over the seas,

Then you and I are sisters' sons:
No better kindred there never could be'.

12 So they sheathed their swords and without delay
Into the tavern they went straight way;
And at the tavern they all did dine,
Where they cracked their bottles and drinked their wine.

Then bold Robin Hood was standing by ...: Vaughan Williams gives a variant for this verse, with the music: 'And Robin Hood was standing by,/And laughing ready to crack his sides,/Saying, 'I'd fight a man as large again,/Before a coward I would ever be'.
Gamble Goff: perhaps originally Gamelyn, the hero of a medieval tale

22   The Fisherman

A great deal has been written about this ballad, which is better known as 'The Bold Fisherman'. Lucy Broadwood suggests that it carries elements of Gnostic symbolism and may be 'a vulgar and secularised transmission of a medieval allegorical original' (*Journal of the Folk Song Society*, 1915, pp.132–5). However, Roger de V. Renwick argues, perhaps more plausibly, that it is simply a returning lover at first unrecognised, a well loved and well worn theme (*English Folk Poetry*, 1980, p.23 ff.). Whichever the case, the language has impressive solemnity and dignity, and the song was widely known. It was one of eighteen sung to Vaughan Williams by James Punt of East Horndon.

As I walked out — one May — mor-ning, — Down by the ri - ver - side, And there I saw — a fish - er - man — Come ro - wing down — the tide.

2 'Good morning to you, fisherman,
   Good morning, sir, I pray,
   For calling you a fisherman
   Just by the break of day'.

3 Then he rowed his boat unto the shore
   And tied it to a stake.
   He stepped up to this gay lady
   And hold of her did take.

4 And he pulled off his morning gown
   And spread it on the ground;
   And there she saw three chains of gold
   All from his neck hung down.

5 Down on her bended knees did fall:
   'Oh, pardon, sir, on me
   For calling you a fisherman,
   Come rowing on the sea'.

6 'Rise up, rise up, my pretty maid,
   And come along with me.
   There's not one word that you have said
   The least offended me.

7 'I'll take you to my father's house
   And married we shall be;
   And you shall have a fisherman
   To row you on the sea'.

23   Keepers and Poachers

'You subjects of England come listen awhile,/Here is a new ditty may
cause you to smile./It is of the King and a Keeper also/Who met in a
Forrest some winters ago': so begins a ballad of about 1696, entitled
'The Loyal Forrister; or, Royal Pastime: being a pleasant Discourse
between the King and a loyal Keeper'. In it, King William goes hunting
his own deer incognito, and is challenged by a keeper, who refuses to be
bribed to let him go. The King then reveals his true identity, and rewards
the faithful servant. This public relations piece for the House of Orange
remains in oral tradition to this day, and some time during the
nineteenth century it produced an off-shoot, usually called either

'William Taylor' (from its hero's name) or 'The Keepers and Poachers'. This in turn survived – and without benefit of print – until the twentieth century, often sung to variants of the tune, 'Villikins and his Dinah', which itself first became popular in the 1840s. Like 'Let Caesar live long', the tune for 'The Loyal Forrister', it is in three/four time. Fights between keepers and poachers were not uncommon in the 1830s and 40s, but the incident involving William Taylor has not been documented. What matters is the spirit of the song.

Good peo-ple of Eng-land, come lis-ten a - while. I will sing you a dit - ty_ which will cause you_ to smile, Con - -cer - ning some poach-ers you ve - ry well know, — They fought in a co - vert some win-ters a - go.

2 Oh, when we go in, boys, good luck to our soul [us all],
  Our guns they do rattle, our pheasants do fall;
  Our guns they do rattle, the keepers do say:
  'Begone, my bold fellows, how dare you come nigh?'

3 Says one to another, 'What shall we do?'
  Up spoke another: 'We all must stand true'.
  They all did stand true and they all stood as one;
  They faced the bold keepers, and the battle begun.

4 There was one, William Taylor, did not run away,
  Till five of those keepers all on him did play.
  Young Taylor, being tired, he sat down to rest;
  Young Taylor was taken because he fought the best.

5 O such a brave fellow there never was yet;
  He must suffer to be hanged before he would split.
  He would suffer to be hanged, the keepers well know,
  And he fought in the covert some winters ago.

[39]

24 Merry Green Broom Fields

This sprightly story of a wager lost through witchcraft is at least seven hundred years old. The ballad first appeared in the eighteenth century, and continued to be sold in the streets as a broadside until the end of the nineteenth century. Vaughan Williams's singer was born in about 1827. His version is a little threadbare in parts, but has some fine touches. The 'night hawk' of verse 8 recalls the goss-hawk in the text printed by Sir Walter Scott (*Minstrelsy of the Scottish Border*, 1802–3) and others.

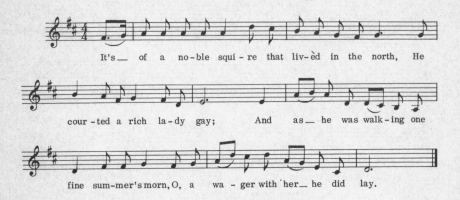

It's— of a no-ble squi-re that liv-èd in the north, He
cour-ted a rich la-dy gay; And as— he was walk-ing one
fine sum-mer's morn, O, a wa-ger with her— he did lay.

2 'A wager, a wager', this lady [did] say,
  'And pray, sir, what might your wager be?
  For if ever I loved you better I never should deny
  That I love to be merry and free'.

3 He said, 'I will lay you a hundred pounds,
  A hundred pounds, aye, and ten,
  That a maiden if you go to the merry green broom fields,
  Then a maiden you will not return again'.

4 So the wager was laid and the money down paid,
  That was paid all down in her father's hall;
  And straightway he goes across the merry green broom fields,
  Where his joy and delight was to call.

5 The weather being pleasant, so pleasant and warm,
  He lay himself down for to sleep;
  And as he lay sleeping his true love came by,
  And great notice of him [she] did take.

6 Nine times she walked [round] the sole of his feet,
  And ten times the crown of his head;

[40]

Nine times she kissed his red cherry cheek,
As he lay sleeping on the green mossy bank.

7 She gathered him a nosegay as sweet as rose in June,
And laid it all underneath his hair,
So that [when] he was woken right out of his sleep
He was sure that his love had been there.

8 He callèd out for his little night hawk
That mounts in the air so high:
'Why didn't you wake me out of my sleep
While my joy and delight came by?'

9 'I shruck loud three times, mastèr,
And I hoverèd [all] aloft:
"She is here, she is here, but she soon will be gone",
And surely my wages will be earned.'

10 'Where was you, my little pointer,
With your neck all surrounded with gold?
Why didn't you wake me right out of my sleep,
My joy and delight to behold?'

11 'I barkèd loud three times, mastèr,
And the golden collar round my neck did shake:
"She is here, she is here, but she soon shall be gone",
But no notice of me you did take'.

12 'Where was you, my footman, John,
I dressed up in apparel so fine?
Why didn't you wake me right out of my sleep,
[For] the wages that might have been thine?'

13 'You should sleep a little longer in the night, mastèr,
And not quite so long in the day.
If a fair young damsel come to meet you in the merry green broom field,
For a wager she never went away'.

25   Fountains Flowing

Despite all the entreaties of his interlocutor, whose grief is poignantly and hauntingly expressed, a young man is about to sail away. He appears to be going to war; if so, his idea of it ('everlasting joy and fountains flowing') is very strange indeed. Vaughan Williams made one version of the tune for this song nationally known by adapting it to John Bunyan's poem, 'To be a Pilgrim'.

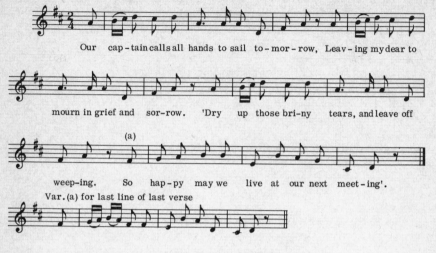

Our cap-tain calls all hands to sail to-mor-row, Leav-ing my dear to mourn in grief and sor-row. 'Dry up those bri-ny tears, and leave off weep-ing. So hap-py may we live at our next meet-ing'.

Var. (a) for last line of last verse

2 'How can you go abroad fighting those strangers?
   You'd better stay at home free from all dangers.
   I'll hold you in my arms, my dearest jewel,
   So stay at home with me, love, and don't be cruel.

3 'When I had gold in store I found you liked me;
   And now I'm lone and poor you seem to slight me.
   You courted me awhile just to deceive me;
   Now my poor heart you have won, you're going to leave me'.

4 Down on the ground she fell like one a-dying,
   Wringing her hands abroad, weeping and sighing:
   'There is no b'lief in man, not your own brother,
   So girls if you must love, love one another'.

5 I said: 'Goodbye, my dear father and mother.
   I am your only child, I have no brother,
   But don't you weep for me, for I am going
   To everlasting joy and fountains flowing'.

The Jolly Harrin'

Salt herring was for centuries a cheap item of diet for the poor. However, the earliest printing of the song seems to have been in 1895, though a manuscript copy was taken down as early as 1831. Even so, this is a very late date for a song 'whose earliest connections were probably with that central agrarian rite involving a sacrifice, human or other, at some critical time of the farming calendar, aimed at the regeneration of natural forces' (A.L. Lloyd, *Folk Song in England*, 1967, p.93). Folklorists love to see traces of ancient ritual in songs and customs, some of which have little in the way of proven ancestry. If ever there were immemorial solemnity in 'The Jolly Harrin' ', it is not there now, and we are left with a jovial and jumbled catalogue of lying exaggeration. The words italicised were spoken.

VERSE 1

1. As I was a walk-ing out one May morn-ing down by the ri-ver-side, _____ There I spied a jol-ly har-rin' come row-ing down by the tide. _____ That was for-ty feet wide and fif-ty feet long, Don't you think that was a jol-ly har-rin'? _____

VERSE 2

2. O what do you think I made with his *head*? There was o-ver ten loaves of bread, There was ten loaves of bread and o-ther fine things. Don't you think I did well with my jol-ly har-rin'? _____

[43]

VERSES 3 - 7

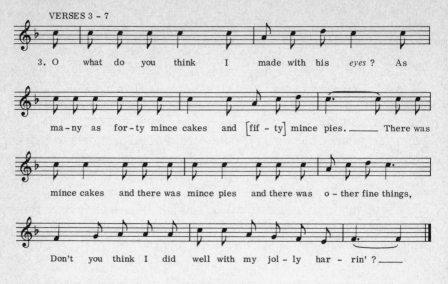

3. O what do you think I made with his *eyes* ? As

ma-ny as for-ty mince cakes and [fif - ty] mince pies. ____ There was

mince cakes and there was mince pies and there was o - ther fine things,

Don't you think I did well with my jol - ly har - rin' ? ____

4 O what do you think I made with his *back*?
   As many half crowns and shillings as you could put in a sack.
   There was half crowns and there was shillings and there was other fine things.
   Don't you think, *etc.*

5 O what do you think I made of his *ribs*?
   As many as forty sheep racks and fifty cow cribs.
   There was sheep racks and there was cow cribs and there was other fine
       things.
   Don't you think, *etc.*

6 O what do you think I made with his *guts*?
   As many as forty pretty maids and fifty nasty sluts.
   There was pretty maids and there was nasty sluts and there was other fine
       things.
   Don't you think, *etc.*

7 O what do you think I made with his *tail*?
   As many little ships as ever set sail.
   There was a great ship, there was a little ship, there was a boat to row in.
   Don't you think, *etc.*

27   The Buffalo

Our perception of American life is now rather different from the frontier idyll portrayed here, and the song is distinctly rare. It is said to date from the early eighteenth century, but the earliest copies that I have seen come from the early nineteenth.

Come all ___ you young fel - lows that have a mind to roam Un - to some fo - reign coun - try, your sta - tion for to change. Un - to some fo - reign coun - try a - way from here we'll go, We'll lay down on the banks ___ of the plea - sant O - hi - o, ___ ___ the plea - sant O - hi - o. Through the wild ___ woods we'll wan - der and chase the buf - fa - lo.

2 There are fishes in the river that are fitting for our use,
  And fine lofty sugar-canes that yield us fine juice;
  And all sorts of game, my boys, besides the buck and doe.
  Through the wild woods, *etc.*

3 Come all you young maidens and spin us some yarn,
  To make us some clothing to keep ourselves warm,

For you can card and spin, my girls, while we can reap and mow.
Through the wild woods, *etc.*

4 Suppose those wild Indians should chance to come near,
  We'll all unite together, boys, free from all care;
  We'll go into the town, my boys, and fire the fatal blow.
  Through the wild woods, *etc.*

28   Elwina of Waterloo

The battle of Waterloo inspired a whole crop of ballads, some martial
and some sentimental; some well known and some rarely heard. This is
in the latter category in both instances: although it turns up once or
twice on broadsides, the version noted by Vaughan Williams from a
Hampshire man in Salisbury Almshouses seems to be unique.

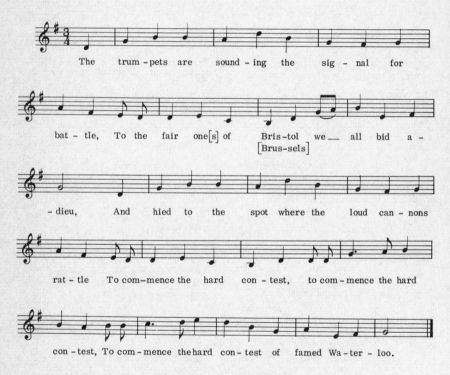

The trum-pets are sound-ing the sig-nal for bat-tle, To the fair one[s] of Bris-tol [Brus-sels] we all bid a-dieu, And hied to the spot where the loud can-nons rat-tle To com-mence the hard con-test, to com-mence the hard con-test, To com-mence the hard con-test of famed Wa-ter-loo.

2 As wounded I lay while the battle was raging
  A maiden most charming appeared to my view.
  So blooming in beauty, so sweetly engaging

Was the lovely Elwina, was the lovely Elwina,
Was the lovely Elwina of famed Waterloo.

3 So sweet was the lily, so modestly bending,
And sweet were the violets in blossom so blue.
More fairer and sweeter was my lovely befriended,
The lovely Elwina, *etc.*

4 I reclined on her arm one morning to lead me
Across the damp meadows so dismal to view.
I tenderly pressed that sweet maiden to wed me,
So I brought that sweet flower, I brought that sweet flower,
I brought that sweet flower from famed Waterloo.

was my lovely befriended: 'the wounded befriending was . . .' (broadside)

29   Long Lankin; or, Young Lambkin

This ballad has an ancient resonance, though the earliest English text
was taken down only in 1775. In versions deriving from Scotland (for an
example of which, see my *Everyman's Book of British Ballads*, 1980, no
55) there is normally an introductory verse which gives the reason for
the ensuing savagery: the lord has failed to pay the mason for building
his castle. Vaughan Williams's source was a Mrs Chidell of Bournemouth, 'lately deceased (1905), at an advanced age', who learned this
and other songs from a Mrs H. Waring of Lyme Regis, Dorset, who in
turn came from Somerset. There is no indication of where Mrs Waring
learned the songs. However, her 'Long Lankin' is close to texts from
Northumberland and Northamptonshire given by Child (no 93 F), and
the word 'moss' (verse 1) is chiefly used in the north.

Said my lord to my la - dy as he moun - ted _ his _
horse: 'Be - ware of Long Lan - kin that lives in the moss.'

[47]

2 'Let the doors be all bolted, the windows all pinned,
   And leave not a loophole for Long Lankin to creep in'.

3 So he mounted his horse and he rode away,
   And he was in London before the break of day.

4 And the doors were all bolted, the windows all pinned,
   All but one little loophole where Long Lankin crept in.

5 'Where is the lord of this house?' said Long Lankin.
   'He's away in fair London', said the false nurse to him.

6 'Where is the lady of this house?' said Long Lankin.
   'She's up in her chamber', said the false nurse to him.

7 'Where is the little lord of this house?' said Long Lankin.
   'He's asleep in his cradle', said the false nurse to him.

8 'Then we'll prick him all over and over with a pin,
   And we'll make my lady to come down to him'.

9 So they pricked him all over and over with a pin,
   And the nurse held the basin for the blood to flow in.

10 'Oh, nurse, how you slumber; oh, nurse, how you sleep.
    You leave my little son, Johnson, to cry and to weep.

11 'Oh, nurse, how you slumber; oh, nurse, how you snore.
    You leave my little son, Johnson, to cry and to roar'.

12 'I've tried him with milk and I've tried him with pap.
    Come down, my fair lady, and nurse him in your lap.

13 'I've tried him with onions, I've tried him with pears.
    Come down, my fair lady, and nurse him in your chairs'.

14 'How can I come down? 'Tis late in the night.
    There's no candle burning, nor moon to give light'.

15 'You have three silver mantles, as light as the sun.
    Come down, my fair lady, all by the light of one'.

16 So my lady came down the stairs, fearing no harm.
    Long Lankin stood ready to catch her in his arm.

17 'Oh, spare me, Long Lankin; oh, spare me till twelve o'clock.
    You shall have as much gold as you can carry on your back.

18 'Oh, spare me, Long Lankin; oh, spare me one hour.
    You shall have my daughter, Betsy. She is a fair flower'.

[48]

19 'Where is your daughter, Betsy? She may do some good:
   She can hold the basin to catch your life's blood'.

20 Lady Betsy sat up at her window so high.
   She saw her dear father from London riding by.

21 'Oh, father, oh, father, don't lay the blame on me.
   'Twas the false nurse and Lankin that killed your fair lady'.

22 So Long Lankin was hung on a gibbet so high.
   The false nurse was burnt at a stake close by.

the moss: bog, swamp or morass (O.E.D)
the basin: the superstitious dread of allowing noble blood to be spilt on the ground was apparently more powerful than the inhibition on killing nobles

30 The Constant Lovers

A rich girl – at least in ballads – often marries a poor man for love, in the face of her family's disapproval. Here, the roles are reversed, when a rich man proposes to marry a poor girl. He over-rides his mother's objections to the match, reminding her (in some versions) that she herself was once a servant-maid.

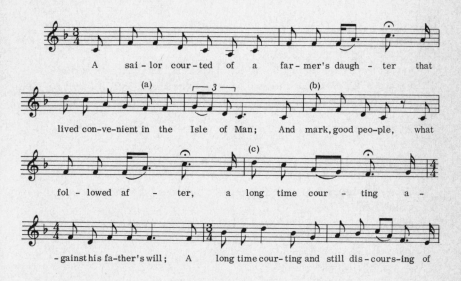

A sai - lor cour - ted of a far - mer's daugh - ter that
lived con - ve - nient in the Isle of Man; And mark, good peo - ple, what
fol - lowed af - ter, a long time cour - ting a -
- gainst his fa - ther's will; A long time cour - ting and still dis - cours - ing of

things con-cern - ing the o-cean wide, He said:'My dar - ling, at

our next meet - ing, if you'll be con-stant, I'll make you my bride'.

Var. (a)   (b)   (c)

(d)

2 'But as for sailors I don't admire them, because they sails in so many parts.
   First they love you and then they slight you, and leave you behind with a
      broken heart.'
   'Don't you say so, my dearest jewel. I never intended to serve you so.
   I have once more to cross the ocean, and you know, my darling, that I must
      go'.

3 The news was carried unto his mother, before he stepped one foot on board,
   That he was courting a farmer's daughter whose aged parents could not
      afford
   One penny portion. Going to the ocean like one distracted, his mother run:
   'If you don't forsake her and your bride not make her, I will disown you to be
      my son'.

4 Oh, when his true love she heard the story, straight to the ocean she then did
      run,
   Saying in a passion, 'You need not mind her. We shall have money when they
      have none'.
   'Money or money not, you are my lot; you have my heart and my free
      goodwill'.
   I won't forsake her, but my bride I'll make her; let my scolding mother say
      what she will.

The Banks of Green Willow

Sailors' superstitions are older than Jonah, who was thrown overboard after being determined by lot as the one causing a tempest which endangered the ship. In the ballad of 'Bonnie Annie' (Child, no 24), of which 'The Banks of Green Willow' is a somewhat confused development, a pregnant woman flees with her lover after robbing her parents, is revealed by lot on ship-board as the cause of a storm, and is cast overboard with her new-born baby. Unlike Jonah, she finds no convenient whale, and her dead body is later washed ashore. Her lover is by no means heartless, but he is powerless to alter the sailors' decision. The singer was the octogenarian, David Clements, of Basingstoke, whose voice Vaughan Williams recorded on a wax cylinder in 1909. Clements repeated each verse.

2 'Oh, it's fetch me some of your father's clothes and some of your mother's
    money,
    That I might go on board a ship with my own dearest honey'.

3 We hadn't been on board a ship but six weeks or better
    Before she wanted women and could not get any.

4 'Oh, it's hold your tongue, oh, you silly girl; oh, it's hold your tongue, my
    honey,
    For we cannot get the women for love nor for money'.

5 I tied a napkin round her head, I tied it round softly,
    And I threw her right over, both she and her baby.

6 I got out upon the deck for to see my love in the water,
    Seeing how she doth swim, my boys, seeing how she doth swagger.

7 She will never leave swimming till she come to some harbour.
    Oh, she shall have a coffin if ever she is founded.

8 Oh, she shall have a coffin, and the nails shall shine yellow,
   And my love shall be buried on the banks of green willow.

32   Robin Hood and the Three Squires

In some cases, when he is merely wishing to win friends and influence
people, Robin Hood's fights (as in no 20) lead to gracious defeats.
When, however, he encounters a genuine enemy – and who could be a
more genuine enemy than the Sheriff of Nottingham himself? – there can
be no question of his coming off second best. The version of this ballad
collected by Vaughan Williams from 75-year-old Mrs Goodyear of
Axford omits after verse 9 Robin's exchange of clothes with a beggar,
his journey to Nottingham, offer to act as hangman for the three squires,
and summons by bugle-blast of one hundred and ten of his merry men.
One broadside has this pleasant coda: 'Then Robin Hood shot a fat
buck,/And Little John shot a fat doe;/Now they are gone to the merry
Sherwood/With the three squires all in a row'. The tune here is more
usually found with 'The Outlandish Knight'.

Bold   Ro - bin Hood rang-èd   the   for - est   all   round, The

for - est all round rang-èd he; _____ And the   first that he   met was a

gay__ la - dy   Come   weep - ing a - long the high - way. _____

2 'Oh, why do you weep, my gay lady;
   Oh, why do you weep?' said he.
   'Oh, why do you weep, my gay lady?
   I pray thee come tell unto me.

3 'Oh, do you weep for gold or fame,
   Or do you weep for me? [fee]
   Or do you weep for anything else
   Belonging to anybody?'

4 'I don't weep for gold or fame,
　　Nor I don't weep for thee;
　　Nor I don't weep for anything else
　　Belonging to anybody'.

5 'Then why do you weep, my gay lady;
　　Why do you weep?' said he.
　　'Oh, why do you weep, my gay lady?
　　I pray thee come tell unto me'.

6 'Oh, I do weep for my three sons,
　　For they are condemned to die'.
　　'Oh, what have they done?' said bold Robin Hood.
　　'Oh, what have they done?' said he.

7 'What parish church have they robbed?' said bold Robin Hood;
　　'Or what parish priest have they slain?
　　Did they ever force a maid against her will,
　　Or with other men's wives have they lain?

8 'Oh, what have they done?' said bold Robin Hood.
　　'Oh, what have they done?' said he.
　　'They have stolen sixteen of the king's white deer.
　　Tomorrow they are condemned to die'.

9 'Go your way home, my gay lady;
　　Go your way home', said he.
　　'Oh, go your way home, my gay lady.
　　Tomorrow I set them free'.

10 'What men are those', said bold Robin Hood [the master sheriff];
　　'What men are all those?' said he.
　　'They are all of them mine and none of them thine.
　　They are come for the squires all three'.

11 'Go and take them, go and take them', says the master sheriff;
　　'Go and take them all,' says he.
　　'Never no more [man] in fair Nottingham town
　　Shall borrow three more of me'.

33　　　Fare ye well, Lovely Nancy

'With sighs and tears this Damsel said, "If you resolve to go to sea,/In Sailor's Robes I'll be array'd, and freely go along with thee"./... Cried

[53]

he, "My Dearest, stay on land, such idle fancies ne'er pursue,/Thy soft and tender milk-white hand Seaman's labour cannot do".' Thus runs a ballad of about 1690, entitled 'The Undaunted Seaman, who resolved to fight for his King and Country; together with his Love's Sorrowful Lamentation at their (sic) Departure', which seems to be the source of various later songs. In 'Jemmy [or William], the Sailor's Adieu', beginning 'adieu, my dearest Nancy', a woman tries to dissuade a sailor from leaving, but he points out that his ship is all ready for sea, at Spithead, with guns loaded, professes his constancy, and departs. The woman does not offer to go to sea with him, as she does in 'William and Nancy's Parting', when he declines to expose her to the dangers of battle and the hardships of shipboard life: 'Your pretty little fingers that are so long and small,/You'd think it hard usage our cable ropes to haul'. Our song includes both the lamentation at parting and the woman's offer to go to sea. It was known to the poet, John Clare, and was a favourite both with sailors and landsmen for the next hundred years. The acerbic conclusion found here is not usual.

[54]

2 'Oh, 'tis not talk of leaving me, my dearest Johnny,
  Oh, 'tis not talk of leaving me here all alone;
  For it is your good company that I do admire:
  I will sigh till I die if I ne'er see you more.

3 'In sailor's apparel I'll dress and go with you,
  In the midst of all dangers your friend I will be;
  And that is, my dear, when the stormy wind's blowing,
  True love, I'll be ready to reef your top sails'.

4 'Your neat little fingers strong cables can't handle,
  Your neat little feet to the topmast can't go;
  Your delicate body strong winds can't endure.
  Stay at home, lovely Nancy, to the seas do not go'.

5 Now Johnny is sailing and Nancy bewailing;
  The tears down her eyes like torrents do flow.
  Her gay golden hair she's continually tearing,
  Saying, 'I'll sigh till I die if I ne'er see you more'.

6 Now all you young maidens by me take warning,
  Never trust a sailor or believe what they say.
  First they will court you, then they will slight you;
  They will leave you behind, love, in grief and in pain.

34   Jockey and Jenny

In dialogues between rustic lovers the protagonists are often called by
these names, especially in songs of Scots origin. Sometimes in England
they become John and Joan, though in the best known example, 'Jockey
and Jenny's Trip to the Fair' (abbreviated to 'Jockey to the Fair') the
earlier conjunction remains. Here, the dialogue is less between the two
lovers than between one of them and an unspecified kinsman who warns
of the disadvantages of marriage. The singer could not recall the first
two lines of the last verse.

Oh, Jock-ey cour-ted Jen-ny all in the height of spring. Oh,
Jock-ey would give a-ny-thing that Jen-ny's heart could win. With her

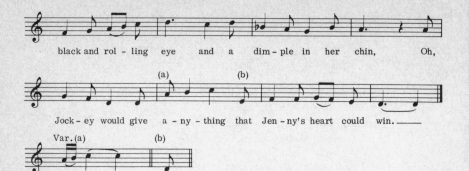

black and rol - ling eye and a dim - ple in her chin, Oh,

(a)　　　　　　　(b)

Jock - ey would give a - ny - thing that Jen - ny's heart could win. ____

Var. (a)　　　(b)

2 'I'll go all through my kinsmen, I'll ask them their advice,
   Whether I should marry you or live a single life'.
   'Oh, kinsman, oh, kinsman, I advise you for the best,
   For whilst a man's a bachelor a single life's the best.

3 'For when a man gets married he must provide a house,
   Likewise a cage to keep a bird and a trap to catch a mouse.
   Here's feather beds, here's bolsters, and everything beside,
   But whilst a man's a bachelor there is nothing to provide.

4 '. . . . .
   . . . .
   Here's spoons, pans and platters, and everything beside,
   But whilst a man's a bachelor there's nothing to provide'.

35　　　　　God Bless the Master

This *quête* song, with its references to Christ's passion, seems to have
started life as an Easter or May carol. However, two verses have been
added at some stage which have brought it into the Christmas season.
They have been borrowed, consciously or otherwise, from a version of
'God rest you, merry gentlemen' (for which see *The Oxford Book of
Carols* – of which Vaughan Williams was one of the editors – no 12).

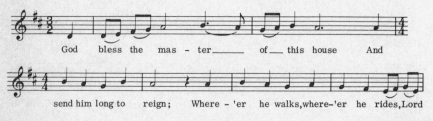

God bless the mas - ter____ of __ this house And
send him long to reign; Where - 'er he walks, where-'er he rides, Lord

Je - sus be his guide, Lord _ Je - sus be his guide.

2 God bless the mistress of this house,
   With a gold chain round her breast;
   Amongst her friends and kindered,
   God send her soul to rest.

3 From morn to morn [Good man, good man], remember thou,
   When first our Christ was born,
   He was crucified between two thieves,
   And crownèd with the thorn.

4 From morn to morn, remember thou,
   When Christ laid on the rood,
   'Twas for our sins and wickedness
   Christ shed his precious blood.

5 God bless the ruler of this house
   And send him long to reign;
   And many a merry Christmas
   We may live to see again.

6 Now I've said my carol,
   Which I intend to do,
   God bless us all both great and small,
   And send us a happy New Year.

36   Pretty Nancy

Another Nancy is left behind by another sailor, this time called William, who tells us in fine lyric vein what he proposes to write to her of the dangers of the seas. Nancy hails from Yarmouth, though she should not be confused with the lady of the same name and town who meets her death in 'The Yarmouth Tragedy'. Other versions have Plymouth or Weymouth, and no doubt further variations, in two syllables, but 'Pretty Nancy of London, in Leadenhall Street' seems to be the *ur-text*. It occurs in *Lord Anson's Garland*, which dates from about 1757.

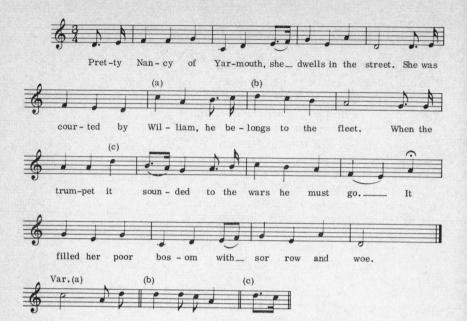

Pret-ty Nan-cy of Yar-mouth, she— dwells in the street. She was
(a)   (b)
cour-ted by Wil-liam, he be-longs to the fleet. When the
(c)
trum-pet it soun-ded to the wars he must go.—— It
filled her poor bos-om with— sor row and woe.
Var.(a)   (b)   (c)

2 'Oh, William, dear William, this will break my heart,
   Since you and I, love, for ever must part.
   You're a-going to those wars, love, where loud cannons roar,
   Where I never, no never, shall see you any more'.

3 'Oh, Nancy, dear Nancy', these words he did say,
   'Our ship she lies anchored and I must away'.
   As he kissed her red, rosy cheeks, from his eyes tears did fall,
   When he bid his dear Nancy adieu and farewell.

4 Then our bold captain he showed us a mark;
   The mark that he showed us it appeared in the dark.
   It came roaring like thunder, and the lightning flash flew,
   All on the salt seas where the stormy winds blow.

5 This is a kind letter I'm going to write
   To Nancy, my charming, my joy and delight.
   It is to inform you what we undergo,
   All on the salt seas where the stormy winds blow.

6 Then up speaks our captain, a well-speaking man:
   'Come, all my bold heroes, here's to old Engeland,
   For the soldiers they will skip, my boys, at the sound of the drum,
   Whilst we poor sailors meets a watery tomb'.

Nelson's Monument

Daniel Wigg, the singer of this song, was born only twenty years after Nelson's death in 1805. Among the many street ballads circulating during his youth was 'Nelson's Monument', and a copy of this has been used to complete his text, since Vaughan Williams took down only the first verse, commenting: 'The rest of the words are not worth printing.' He seems to have repented later, for he preserved in his scrapbook another set forwarded by a correspondent, William Fiske.

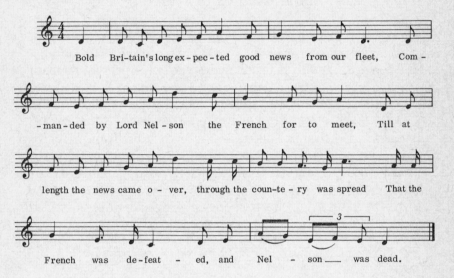

Bold Bri-tain's long ex-pec-ted good news from our fleet, Com-
-man-ded by Lord Nel-son the French for to meet, Till at
length the news came o - ver, through the coun-te-ry was spread That the
French was de-feat - ed, and Nel - son — was dead.

2 Not only brave Nelson, but thousands were slain
   By fighting the French on the watery main;
   To protect England's glory, its honours and wealth,
   We fought and would not yield, till we yielded unto death.

3 The merchants of Yarmouth, hearing us say so,
   Said, 'Come, dearest brothers, to church let us go,
   And there we will build a most beautiful pile,
   In remembrance of Nelson, the hero of the Nile'.

4 'Your plan', says Britannia, 'is exceedingly good:
   A monument for Nelson, a sword for Collingwood.
   Let it be of polished marble to perpetuate his name,
   And in letters of gold, write: "He died for England's fame".'

5 All seamen and soldiers, as I have been told,
   They've ordered themselves in readiness to hold;

Their rights to maintain, their cause to support,
From any invasion keep each British port.

6 Both soldiers and sailors, mighty deeds they have done;
Their arms in foreign parts many battles have won.
If the Nile could but speak or Egypt declare,
All the world with Lord Nelson they could not compare.

38   The Lowlands of Holland

A young man is forcibly removed from his betrothed, and compelled to
go to sea. The woman's parents are not entirely displeased, and urge a
different match, but their daughter makes vows of austerity, culminating
in a pledge never to marry another. The version sung by William Bone of
Medstead, near Alton, is very close to the broadside entitled 'Maiden's
Complaint for the Loss of Her Sailor', printed between 1802 and 1819
by John Pitts, 14 Great St Andrew Street, Seven Dials. This derives from
'The Lowlands of Holland', which was originally about a man forced to
fight with the army in Flanders, probably early in the seventeenth
century, though the earliest printings did not appear until the 1760s.
Whatever its origin, the song is a moving expression of intense grief.

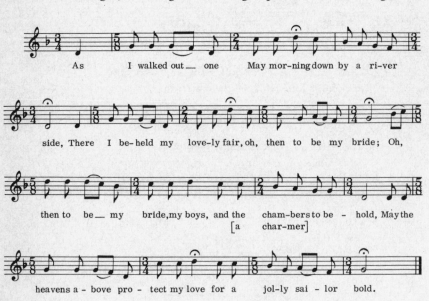

[60]

2 I will build my love a gallant ship, a ship of noble fame,
   With a hundred and seventy sailor boys to box her about the main;
   To box her about the main, my boys, without any fear or doubt.
   With my true love in the gallant ship I was sadly tossed about.

3 Said the father to the daughter, 'What makes you so lament?
   There is a lad in our town can give your heart content'.
   'There is not a lad in our town, neither lord nor duke', said she,
   'Since the raging sea and stormy winds parted my love and me.

4 'No handkerchief shall bind my head, no comb go through my hair.
   No firelight nor candle bright shall view my beauty rare;
   And neither will I married be until the day I die,
   Since the raging sea and stormy winds parted my love and I'.

5 The anchor and the cable went overboard straightway;
   The mainmast and the rigging laid buried in the sea:
   'Twas tempests and bad weather and the raging of the sea.
   I never had but one true love, and he was drowned at sea.

to box her about: to sail up and down
I will build ... With my true love ... I was sadly tossed: most versions have:
   They did build ... And my true love ... he was ...

39   The Drowned Sailor

Here is another song, fairly popular in the early twentieth century, which had its origin well over two hundred years earlier. Francis Digby had a mistress, the Duchess of Richmond, with whom he was passionately in love. When he had to sail away to fight the Dutch in 1671 the parting was celebrated in a poem by John Dryden (later made into a street ballad) and also in a ballad, both of which were entitled 'Captain Digby's Farewell'. Two years later the three-verse ballad was lengthened and re-issued to commemorate the death of the Earl of Sandwich, which took place when his ship, the *Royal George* (for which, see no 80) was destroyed by the Dutch in the Battle of Southwold Bay. The Earl's drowned body was found a few days after the battle. 'The Sorrowful Ladie's Complaint' (1673) deals with her grief at finding her lover's body on the sea-shore. The song continued to circulate, partly thanks to a number of broadside printings, in which the tragic scene was often moved to Yorkshire, either to Scarborough Sands or Robin Hood's Bay, six miles south of Whitby.

In Lon-don fair ci-ty a dam-sel did dwell. She was cour-ted by a sai-lor, and he lov-èd her well; And he pro-mised for to mar-ry her if he e-ver did re-turn, By the marks on his for-tune all on him did stand.
[But mark what hard] [them] [run.]

2 As he was a-sailing along so brave
Those winds and those waves began for to rise.
The storm it was-arising and the billows loud did roar,
Which tossed this young sailor all on the seashore.

3 As she was a-walking down by the sea-sung [sea strand]
She saw her drownded sailor lie dead on the ground;
And when she came near him he put her to a stand:
She knew 'twas her true love by the marks on his hand.

4 She kissed him, she hugged him, she called him her dear;
Ten thousand times over she kissèd him there,
Saying, 'I'm very well contented, love, to lie by your side.
My green grave shall be instead of a new married life'.

5 As she was a-walking down by the sea-side
And wringing of her tender hands, so bitterly did cry,
Saying, 'My joys are all ended, my sorrows are all fled'.
In a few moments after this young damsel died.

6 In Robin Hood's churchyard this couple was buried,
And all for a memorandum [monument] a tombstone was laid.
Come all you constant lovyers that here do pass by,
See this unfortunate couple, how happy they do lie.

HEREFORDSHIRE

40   Riding Down to Portsmouth

A sailor on his way to Portsmouth spends the night at an inn with a
prostitute. As a result he is robbed of his watch and money, left to pay
the bill, and into the bargain given a dose of venereal disease. This racy
story was sung to a lively tune by Esther Smith, a gypsy living near
Weobley in Herefordshire. (Vaughan Williams also collected from her
mother, Mrs Whatton; her daughter, May Bradley, sang for Fred Hamer
in the 1960s.) 'Riding Down to Portsmouth' is extremely uncommon in
print. Even so, Vaughan Williams did not take down the words, so I
have supplied them from a rare broadside printed by William M'Call of
Liverpool.

2 She says, 'Kind sir, if I go along with you, I am sure I must be married'.
  She said, 'Kind sir, if I go along with you, I'm sure I must be carried'.
  So she went with him straightway and slept in his arms till next day,
  And she left him all the reckoning to pay, riding down to Portsmouth.

3 It was in the morning she awoke and found him snoring.
  Thus to herself she did say: 'He shall pay for his whoring.
  For the money he ain't spent in wine, the rest of it shall be mine,
  And his gold watch, too, I'll have besides, in riding down to Portsmouth'.

4 Early in the morning he awoke and found his lady missing.
  These words to himself he did say: 'I have paid for my kissing,
  For she's robbed me of my gold watch and purse, and singed me which is ten
      times worse.
  Sure, I must have lain under a curse, in riding down to Portsmouth.

5 'Oh, landlord, tell me what I have to pay, that I may reward you.
  Oh, landlord, tell me what I have to pay, that I may regard you;
  And my horse I will leave here in pawn till back from sea I do return,
  And all such gallows ones I'll shun, in riding down to Portsmouth'.

41   On Christmas Day

A vengeful and even cruel attitude is expressed in this carol, which is far
removed from the conventional view of Christmas.

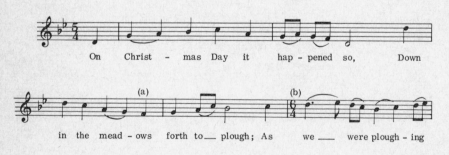

[64]

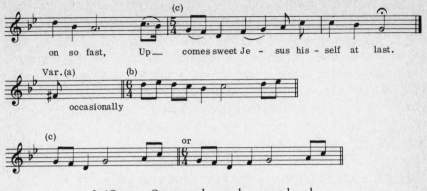

on so fast, Up— comes sweet Je - sus his - self at last.

2 'O man, O man, what makes you plough
   So hard upon the Lord's birthday?'
   The farmer answered him with great speed:
   'For the plough this day we have great need'.

3 His arms did quaver to and fro;
   His arms did quaver, he could not plough.
   The ground did open and lose him in,
   Before he could repent of sin.

4 His wife and children are out of place,
   His beasts and cattle they die away;
   His beasts and cattle they die away,
   For the breaking of our Lord's birthday.

His: variant: my (verse 4)   *out of place:* out of work

42   Dives and Lazarus

'Mrs Phillips took me into the parlour where I sat down, took a leaf out
of my pocket book and wrote with my address a request that Phillips
would send me by post 1. the song about our Saviour, 2. the song about
Lazarus, 3. the song about King James and the Tinker. Mrs Phillips
brought me a pint of excellent light bright beer, some sweet homebaked
bread, and some cheese.' Thus Parson Kilvert, after a visit to the *Sun Inn*
at Colva on 26 February, 1870. A few days later he duly received copies
of the first two ('imperfect but very curious and of some merit'), though
the words of the third had been forgotten. Kilvert was so impressed that
on a visit to Hay Castle (3 March): 'I read aloud to them my Colva
Ballads which interested them much.' Unfortunately, the texts have not

survived in Kilvert's papers. The first was conceivably a version of 'The Bitty Withy' (for which, see no 44), since Kilvert elsewhere calls it 'the ballad of our Saviour and the Three Children'. The second, 'Dives and Lazarus', deriving from the powerful parable in Luke, chapter 16, had been popular since Elizabethan times, the first printed version having appeared in 1557. By about 1616 a character in *The Nice Valour*, by Fletcher and Massinger, could casually mention 'church corners, where *Dives* and the suff'ring Ballads hang'. In the eighteenth and nineteenth centuries there seems to have been intense interest in carols in the West Midlands, where they were widely printed and frequently sung. Vaughan Williams reaped a particularly good harvest in Herefordshire, less than forty years after Kilvert's time. He was enthralled by 'Dives': 'When I hear the fifth variation of the "Enigma" series I feel the same sense of familiarity, the same sense of something peculiarly belonging to me as an Englishman which I also felt when I first heard "Bushes and Briars" [no 16] or "Lazarus" ' (*National Music*, 1934, p.76).

[As it] fell out up-on one day Rich Di-vus made a— feast, And

(a)

he in-vi-ted all his friends And gen-try of the best.

Var.(a)

2 Then Lazarus laid him down and down,
   And down at Dives' door:
   'Some meat, some drink, brother Dives,
   Bestow upon the poor'.

3 'Thou art none of my brother, Lazarus,
   That lies begging at my door.
   No meat nor drink I'll give thee,
   Nor none I'll bestow on the poor'.

4 Then Lazarus laid him down and down,
   And down at Dives' wall:
   'Some meat, some drink, brother Dives,
   Or with hunger starve I shall'.

5 'Thou art none of my brother, Lazarus,
   That lies begging at my wall.
   No meat nor drink I'll give to thee,
   But with hunger starve you shall'.

6 Then Lazarus laid him down and down,
   And down at Dives' gate:
   'Some meat, some drink, brother Dives,
   For Jesus Christ his sake'.

7 'Thou art none of my brother, Lazarus,
   That lies begging at my gate.
   No meat nor drink I'll give to thee,
   For Jesus Christ his sake'.

8 Then Dives sent out his merry men
   To whip poor Lazarus away,
   But they had no power to strike a stroke,
   And threw their whips away.

9 Then Dives sent out his hungry dogs
   To worry poor Lazarus away,
   But they had no power to bite one bite,
   So they licked his sores away.

10 As it fell out upon a day,
   Poor Lazarus sickened and died.
   There came two angels out of heaven,
   His soul there to guide.

11 'Rise up, rise up, brother Lazarus,
   And come along with me;
   For there's a place in heaven provided,
   To sit on an angel's knee'.

12 As it fell out upon a day
   That Dives sickened and died,
   There came two serpents out of hell,
   His soul there to guide.

13 'Rise up, rise up, brother Dives,
   And come along with me;
   For there's a place in hell provided,
   To sit on a serpent's knee'.

14 Then Dives lifted up his eyes
   And saw poor Lazarus blest:

'A drop of water, brother Lazarus,
For to quench my flaming thirst.

15 'If I had as many years to live
As there is blades of grass,
I would make it in my will secure
That the devil should have no power.

16 'Oh, hell is dark, oh, hell is deep;
Oh, hell is full of mice.
It is a pity that any poor sinful soul
Should depart from our saviour, Christ'.

17 And now my carol's ended,
No longer can I stay.
God bless you all, both great and small,
And God send you a happy New Year.

Dives: 'Mr Evans sang and wrote
consistently: Divus' (note by
Vaughan Williams).
serpent's knee: a much derided
phrase, sometimes replaced by 'For
wicked men like thee'

full of mice: should probably be
'mist', with which the word
'Christ' would have rhymed in
Middle English

43   The Carnal and the Crane

We are told that carnal derives from the French, *corneille*, and means
crow. However, the word seems to have been used nowhere but in this
ballad, which was first printed early in the nineteenth century. William
Hone places it twelfth in his list of 89 'Christmas Carols now annually
Printed' (*Ancient Mysteries Described*, 1823, p.97). He mentions a
version 'still sung' in Warwickshire which has 'marks of age', including
the use of 'the obsolete word *rein*, formerly used in the sense of *run*'
(p.93). The ballad is full of Biblical tales, some apocryphal, summed up
by Child as: 'the birth and earliest days of Jesus: the Immaculate
Conception; the Nativity; the conference of Herod with the Wise Men,
including the miracle of the roasted cock; the Flight into Egypt, with the
Adoration of the Beasts and the Instantaneous Harvest; the Massacre of
the Innocents'. This version contains only some of these incidents.

[68]

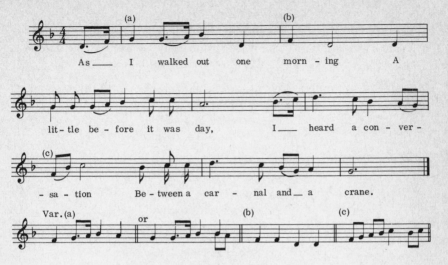

As — I walked out one morn - ing A
lit - tle be - fore it was day, I — heard a con - ver -
- sa - tion Be - tween a car - nal and — a crane.

Var. (a) or (b) (c)

2 The carnal said unto the crane:
'If all the world should turn;
But once we had a father,
But now we have a son'.

3 There was a star all in the east
Shone out a-shining throng, [strong?]
And shone in King Pharaoh's chamber,
And where King Pharaoh lay.

4 The wise men they soon spied it,
And soon King Pharaoh told
That an earthly babe was born that night
As no man on earth could destroy.

5 King Pharaoh sent for his armèd men,
And ready then they be,
For all children under two years old
Shall be slainèd, they shall be.

6 Joseph and Mary
Was weary of their rest;
They travelled into Egypt,
Into the Holy Land.

7 'Go speed thy work', said Joseph,
'Go fetch thy oxen wain,
And carry home thy corn again
As which this day hath sown.

[69]

8 'If anyone should ask you
   Whether Jesus he has passed by,
   You can tell them Jesus he did pass by
   Just as your seeds were sown'.

9 Then up came King Pharaoh
   With his armèd men so bold,
   Enquiring of the husbandman
   Whether Jesus he has passed by.

10 'The truth it must be spoken,
   The truth it must be told:
   I saw Jesus passing by
   Just as my seeds were sown'.

11 King Pharaoh said to his armèd men:
   'Your labour and mine's in vain;
   It's full three-quarters of a year
   Since these seeds were sown'.

44   The Bitter Withy

Although a single verse appeared in 1868, it was not until 1905 that a full version of this carol was available in print. Nevertheless, it seems to be of considerable antiquity, being based on incidents in the apocryphal gospels (*Pseudo-Matthew* and *Thomas*) transposed into an English setting. These in turn have their roots in even earlier stories, Oriental and Celtic.

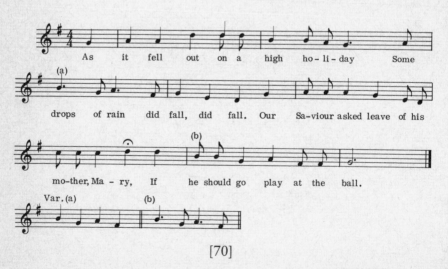

As it fell out on a high ho-li-day Some drops of rain did fall, did fall. Our Sa-viour asked leave of his mo-ther, Ma - ry, If he should go play at the ball.

Var. (a)   (b)

[70]

2 'Go play at the ball, my own dear son,
   'Tis time that you were going or gone;
   And don't let me hear of any complaints
   At night when you come home'.

3 So up Lincorn and down Lincorn
   Our saviour he did run, did run,
   Until he came to the well of fortune,
   Where he met three jolly jordans [lordlings].

4 'Well met, well met, three jolly jordans,
   Your bodies are all safe, I see;
   And which of you three jolly jordans
   Can come play at the ball with me?'

5 'Come play at the ball? We're lords' and ladies' sons,
   Born in a bower all in all;
   And you are only but a poor maiden's child,
   Born in an oxen's stall'.

6 'If you are lords' and ladies' sons,
   Born in a bower all in all,
   I'll make it appear at the very latter end
   That I am above you all'.

7 So our saviour made a bridge of the beams of the sun,
   And over the sea went he;
   And these three jolly jordans followed after him,
   And they were drowned all three'.

8 So up Lincorn and down Lincorn
   Their mothers they did hoot and call,
   Saying: 'Mary mild, call home your child,
   For ours are drownded all'.

9 So Mary mild called home her child,
   And laid him across her tender knee;
   And with a handful of the bitter withy
   She gave him slashes three.

10 'O the withy, the bitter withy,
   Thou caused me to smart, to smart.
   O the withy shall be the very first tree
   That shall perish and die at the heart'.

up Lincorn: up the hill (?); up   *all in all:* and hall
   Lincoln (?)

[71]

The Rocks of Scilly

There have been many shipwrecks on the Isles of Scilly, some of them photographed by the Gibsons and chronicled by John Fowles in *Shipwreck* (1974). Perhaps the most spectacular, long before the age of photography, was the destruction of four homeward bound ships from the fleet of Sir Clowdisley Shovell in 1707. Shovell, who was a very fat man, floated to shore, but was murdered by a local woman who smothered him in sand for the sake of his great emerald ring. His body was later brought back for burial at Westminster Abbey. This song, which was first published in 1802, does not appear to relate to a particular incident; it has verbal reminiscences of several other pieces, including 'Sir Patrick Spens'.

Come all you jol - ly sea - men with a __ cour -age stout and bold, Come list'n a - while un - to my__ song, the __ truth I will un - fold. On the four - teen day__ of Ja - nua-ry last for Ja - mai - ca we set sail, And [did steer all the way as we sailed on_ I __ thought of Pol - ly dear.]

2 We sailed and sailed the salt seas round, to the English Channel came,
  Till at length a dreadful storm began for to rise, too dreadful for to name,
  'All hands aloft', our captain cries, 'and see all things are clear,
  For I am certain sure that a dreadful storm is near'.

3 Then up aloft our boatswain went and gazèd all around.
  He gazèd all around with watery eyes but no land could he espy;
  'O here's a fee of fifty pounds to a man that can see land,
  Here's fifty guineas of bright money I'll pay into his hand'.

4 Now behold there was a brisk young man on the quarter deck did stand,
   Cries, 'Cheer up, cheer up, my lively lads, for behold I can see land'.
   In turning their ship so nimbly about, thinking all danger past,
   All in that very same moment on the Scilly Rocks were cast.

5 The first crack our ship did give, aloud our captain cried:
   'The Lord have mercy on our souls, we in the deep must lie'.
   Out of ninety seamen stout and bold only fourteen came on shore
   To carry the news to pretty Polly dear, she's the girl I do adore.

6 And when the news to London came that our good ship was lost,
   O many a seaman did shed tears to think how she'd been tossed.
   'Where's my love?' cries pretty Polly dear. 'Have you lost my love?' she cried.
   Just like some lily drooping she bowed her head and died.

London: in some versions, 'Plymouth'

46   A Brisk Young Sailor

A woman is seduced, then abandoned, but remains in love with the man
responsible (usually identified simply as a farmer, a soldier, or a sailor).
The song was widespread, under several titles. In 'Sheffield Park', 'Died
for Love', and some versions of 'A Brisk Young Sailor', the woman dies.
'There is an Alehouse' has a jollier vein, and enjoyed a considerable
vogue as 'There is a Tavern in the Town'. Vaughan Williams's singer,
William Colcombe, died in Weobley Workhouse in 1911, at the age of
84. He knew some thirty traditional songs and carols, some of which he
learned in his youth from a Weobley nailmaker known as 'Old Powell'.
Colcombe had the additional distinction of being the last man in his
village to wear a smock-frock.

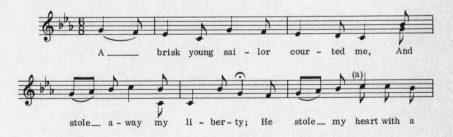

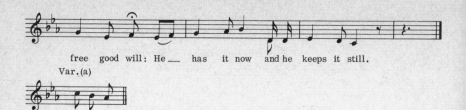

free   good   will: He __ has   it   now   and he   keeps it   still.

Var.(a)

2 Down in the meadow as I did run
   To pick the flowers as they sprung,
   At every sort I gave a pull,
   Until I puck my apurn full.

3 And as I carried my apurn low
   My true love followed, through frost and snow;
   But now a smile I canna win:
   He'll pass me by and say nothin'.

4 Yonder is an alehouse in yon town,
   He'll take a seat and sit himself down;
   He'll take a strange girl on his knee,
   And don't you think that's grief to me?

5 Oh, how grieved I am, how grieved I am,
   For she has gold and I have none;
   But gold will waste and beauty blast:
   This poor girl will come like me at last.

6 There is a rogue on yonder hill,
   He has a heart as hard as steel;
   He has two hearts instead of one,
   And he'll be a rogue when I am gone.

47   The Myrtle Tree

This song seems to have originated as a street ballad, entitled 'Flash
Company', in which a woman bids farewell to her lover as he is on the
point of being transported for some crime, probably theft. They
exchange vows of fidelity, using motifs from other songs, including that
of the myrtle tree growing in the ocean. The myrtle has a very long
history, going back to the Garden of Eden. For the Jews it signified the
bounty of God; for the Greeks it was sacred to Aphrodite and Astarte,
and also stood for immortality. In England it was merely considered

lucky, though here the incongruity and impossibility of its growing in the ocean serves as a powerful gage of fidelity.

'First I loved Tho-mas, but now I love John. Then I loved Ed-win, he's a cle-ver young man. With his white cot-ton stock-ings and his high an-kled shoes, He wears a vel-vet jack-et, like a flash lad he goes'.

Var. (a)

2 'For fiddling and dancing is all my delight,
   And keeping flash company has ruined me quite.
   Ruined me quite, and a great many more;
   If I'd not kept bad company I'd never been so poor'.

3 'Take this yellow handkerchief in remembrance of me,
   And I hope you will wear it in your high company;
   For in the middle of the ocean there shall grow a myrtle tree
   Before ever I prove false to her, to the girl that loves me.'

4 'Here's adieu to you judges and juries, you are too severe;
   You have banished my true love from me I declare'.
   'May the rocks run water and the rivers run dry
   If ever I prove false to the girl that loves I'.

5 'If the wars should come again, love, what would old England say?
   They would wish for the transports they have sent far away.
   They would wish for transports to return back again
   To fight for old England their right to maintain'.

flash: criminal, and also showy

[75]

Vaughan Williams collected at least five tunes for this song, all without words. This is surprising, because Mrs Powell, the singer of the version given here, knew at least one verse, which was communicated to Vaughan Williams by Mrs E. M. Leather: 'A blacksmith courted me, both late and early./A blacksmith courted me, I loved him dearly:/With his hammer in his hand, striking a fire,/I'll go to my true love, that is my desire'. Mrs Powell's tune appeared in *The Penguin Book of English Folk Songs* (edited by R. Vaughan Williams and A. L. Lloyd, 1959, p.22) with a different text, of which Lloyd writes: 'The song was contributed by R.V.W., who had a special liking for it. To the best of my recollection the words are as he wanted, but where he got them, I don't know' (personal communication). The text appears to be an adaptation of broadside number 241, issued by H. Such, 177 Union Street, Borough, London S.E. If this was indeed Vaughan Williams's source, he bowdlerised one line ('when you sat beside me' (verse 4) for 'when by me you did lie'), and omitted the last two verses, of which the final one entirely changes the conclusion of the song, altering it from grief, remorse and despair to something quite different: 'Come all you pretty maids don't you be daunted,/By being left alone – from your lovers parted./Now do as I have done, you will your trouble smother,/And keep your spirits up, you soon will find another'.

2 And where is my love gone, with his cheeks like roses,
   And his good black billycock on, decked with primroses?

I'm afraid the scorching sun will shine and burn his beauty,
And if I was with my love I'd do my duty.

3 Strange news is come to town, strange news is carried,
Strange news flies up and down that my love is married.
I wish them both much joy, though they don't hear me,
And may God reward him well for slighting of me.

4 'What did you promise [me] when you sat beside me?
You said you would marry me, and not deny me'.
'If I said I'd marry you, it was only for to try you,
So bring your witness, love, and I'll not deny you'.

5 'Oh, witness have I none save God Almighty,
And he'll reward you well for slighting of me'.
Her lips grew pale and white, it made her poor heart tremble
To think she loved one, and he proved deceitful.

And if I was with my love I'd do my duty: 'If I was with my lover he'd do his
duty' (Such broadside).

49   The Drowsy Sleeper

A young man goes courting and announces his presence by singing in the
dark under his true love's window. Unfortunately, her parents are also
roused from sleep, and react angrily, especially as they disapprove of the
match. Their daughter spiritedly calls for her dowry so that she can set
off and marry the (somewhat timorous) man she loves. The song, now
rare, was sung on both sides of the Atlantic, and also printed on
broadsides.

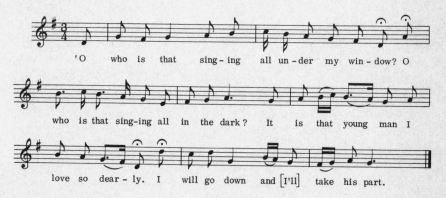

'O who is that sing-ing all un-der my win-dow? O
who is that sing-ing all in the dark? It is that young man I
love so dear-ly. I will go down and [I'll] take his part.

[77]

2 'My mother she does wide awaken.
   My father he can quickly hear.
   He pops his head out of the high room window,
   And then my true love he quickly fled.

3 'Turn back, turn back, do not be a rover.
   Turn back, turn back, for it's almost day,
   And sit you down till your [his] passion's over,
   Then your lawful bride I'll quickly be'.

4 'O daughter, daughter, I'll close confine you,
   All in a room all by your self;
   And you shall live on dry bread and water,
   And once to dine and that's enough'.

5 'I want none of your bread and water,
   Nor nothing else that [to] you belong.
   If I can't attain my own heart's desire,
   Single I will go to my grave.

6 'O father, father, lay down my portion,
   That is five hundred bright pounds in gold,
   Then I may cross yon wide watery ocean
   To leave the dwelling that you do own'.

50   O Who Is That?

A night visit by a lover to his lass via her bedroom window was once an accepted feature of courtship, widely celebrated in European literature and song. English night-visiting songs usually relate the man's arrival, then his request for admittance, which is granted after a conventional show of reluctance. The man departs at dawn, signalled by cock-crow. The earliest printed version seems to be 'John's Earnest Request; or, Betty's compassionate Love extended to him in a time of Distress', which was produced, probably in the 1680s, 'for *P. Brooksby* at the *Golden Ball* in *Pye Corner*', London. In it Betty eventually yields to John's persuasion, and admits him, on promise of marriage. He wins her maidenhead, but does not fail to keep his word. If our fine, lyric song indeed derives from the broadside, it has undergone considerable transformation.

I am a-way, and I can-not tar-ry.

I that ri-ver I will cross. O-ver high hills and

burn-ing moun-tains, un-til I find my own dear lass.

Var.(a)

2 And when I got to my true love's window I leaned low high [gently?] on a
    stone;
  Through a pane of glass I whispered softly: 'My true love, is you now at
    home?'

3 'O who is that at my bedroom window, disturbing me from my night's rest?'
  'Oh who can it be but your true lover, so rise up, darling, and let me in.

4 'I'm wet and weary from my long journey; besides I'm wet unto the skin'.
  So soon did rise that fairest creature, then with prime [speed?] she let me in.

5 O there we warmed our true love together till that long night had been
    drawing nigh [by?]
  Till that long night had been almost morning, I took my liberty and went
    away.

6 Then her white breast like one ice snow [like to snow?] in winter, her two
    bright cheeks like a rose in June,
  Her two bright eyes like stars now a-shining on a winter's night, and I
    freezing came. [it freezes, too?]

Verse 6 seems to belong before verse 5.

51   Wassail Song

Yorkshire and Gloucestershire wassail songs collected by Vaughan
Williams have become nationally known through their inclusion by him

in *The Oxford Book of Carols* (1928, and subsequent editions). The Gloucestershire version was in fact taken down from a Herefordshire singer, as was this unpublished variant.

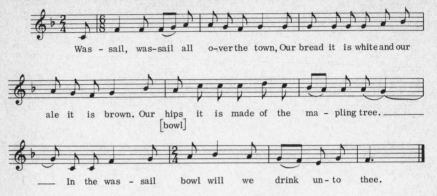

Was - sail, was-sail all o–ver the town, Our bread it is white and our

ale it is brown. Our hips it is made of the ma - pling tree.
[bowl]

— In the was - sail bowl will we drink un - to thee.

2 Here's a health to the ox and to his right eye.
  May God send our master a good Christmas pie,
  A good Christmas pie that we may all see,
  In the wassail bowl will we drink unto thee.

3 Here's a health to the ox and to his right ear.
  May God send our master a happy New Year.
  A happy New Year that we may all see,
  In the wassail bowl, *etc.*

4 Here's a health to the ox and to his right horn.
  May God send our master a good crop of corn.
  A good crop of corn, *etc.*

5 Here's a health to the ox and to his right hip.
  May God send our master a jolly fat sheep.

6 Here's a health to the ox and to his right leg.
  May God send our master a jolly fat hog.

7 Here's a health to the ox and to his right hoof.
  May God send our master a good crop of fruit.

8 Here's a health to the ox and to his fat arse.
  May God send our master a good crop of grass.

9 Here's health to the ox and to his long tail.
  May God send our master a jolly wassail.

[80]

10 Come, butler, come fill us a bowl of the best,
   And I hope your soul in heaven may rest;
   And if you do fill us a bowl of the small,
   May the devil take butler, bowl and all.

11 Come all pretty maidens you were all as one,
   Don't let these wassailers stand out in the cold.
   Step up to the door and pull back the pin,
   And let those jolly wassailers in.

you were all as one: I hope there is one

KENT

52   Orange and Blue

Under the better-known title of 'Green Grows the Laurel' this song is
familiar both in Britain and North America. The words vary considerably, though the verse about exchanging the green laurels for the
orange and blue is always present, and sometimes used as a chorus.
Laurel symbolises young love with its concomitant suffering (rue).
Orange stands for constancy, as does the colour blue. There is a
somewhat implausible theory that the song might have had a covert
political meaning in Ireland, where the green stands for republicanism
(though united with orange and white in the tricolour) and the orange
and blue for Ulster separatism.

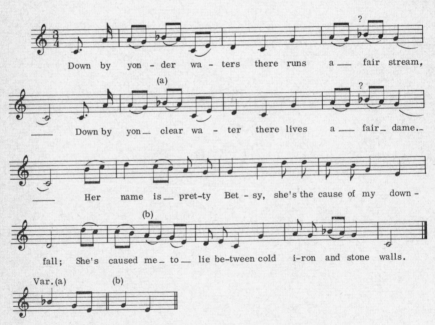

Down by yon-der wa-ters there runs a_ fair stream,
(a)
Down by yon_ clear wa-ter there lives a_ fair_ dame._
Her name is_ pret-ty Bet-sy, she's the cause of my down-
(b)
fall; She's caused me_ to_ lie be-tween cold i-ron and stone walls.
Var.(a)   (b)

2 Her skin's white as paper, her neck is so fair;
   Like a raven's feather so black were her hair.
   She was genteel and handsome where e'er she might go,
   With her hair hanging down her shoulders like ringlets of gold.

[82]

3 I oftentimes wonder why young women love young men;
   I oftentimes have wondered how the men can love them,
   For they are so deceitful as no tongue can tell.
   If ever I love another girl she shall love me as well.

4 Green grow the laurels and so does the rue,
   So sorry was pretty Betsy when we [I] parted from you;
   And at our next meeting our joys we will reward,
   We'll change the green laurels for orange and blue.

NORFOLK

53   The Captain's Apprentice

The plight of pauper children farmed out as apprentices by the poor law guardians caused widespread concern in the late eighteenth and early nineteenth centuries. One thinks of the famous *Memoirs of Robert Blincoe*, which describes the fourteen-year apprenticeship to a Nottinghamshire mill-owner of a boy sent out from St Pancras Workhouse in London at the age of seven, in 1799. At about the same time the death of another pauper apprentice was being chronicled in a fine but bitter song which was sung for another hundred years and more, and still lingers in oral tradition. Vaughan Williams collected it from a septuagenarian fisherman, Mr James Carter, at King's Lynn, and assumed that it was a local production, mainly because of the mention of St James's Workhouse in the town, so called because St James's Chapel had been converted to the use of the poor as early as 1682. However, two verses (5 and 6 here) in Vaughan Williams's scrapbook additional to those sung by Mr Carter (perhaps remembered later by him, and sent on) move the scene to Bristol. This squares with a broadside recently turned up by Mike Yates in the St Bride Institute. It is without imprint, though probably dating from about 1800, and entitled 'A New Copy of Verses, Made on Captain MILLS, now under Confinement in Newgate, at Bristol, for the murder of THOMAS BROWN, his Apprentice Boy'. The account may have been fictional, though there is a record that in 1798 the captain of the *Loyal Briton*, off Minorca, 'killed his Cabin-boy by striking him on the head with a handspike' and 'was ordered back to England for trial' ('The Adventures of Serjeant Benjamin Miller', in *Journal of Army Historical Research,* vol. VII, p.16). A discrepancy in the broadside is its mention of St James's Workhouse, though Bristol Workhouse was called St Peter's Hospital. (However, there is a St James district in Bristol.) Whatever the doubts as to its precise origin, the song held the imagination of singers. It travelled to America, was jotted down in the backs of the logbooks of several whaling ships (see Gale Huntington, *Songs the Whalemen Sang*, New York, 1970), and continued to circulate in England until this century, mainly in Norfolk, but also in Dorset. Vaughan Williams was deeply impressed by Mr Carter's version (though he collected others), and he used the melody or

reminiscences of it in several of his orchestral works, including the
Norfolk Rhapsody, *Sea Symphony* and *Pastoral Symphony*.

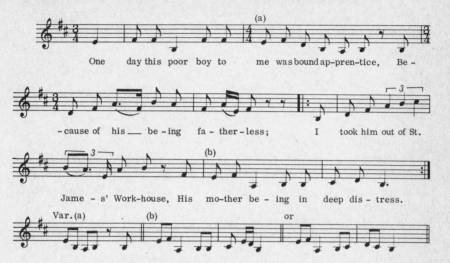

One day this poor boy to me was bound ap-pren-tice, Be-
-cause of his — be-ing fa-ther-less; I took him out of St.
Jame - s' Work-house, His mo-ther be - ing in deep dis - tress.

Var. (a)   (b)   or

2 One day this poor boy unto me offended,
  But nothing to him I did say;
  Up to the main-mast shroud I sent him,
  And there I kept him all that long day.

3 All with my garling-spikk I misused him,
  So shamefully I can't deny;
  All with my marling-spike I gagged him
  Because I could not bear his cry.

4 His face and his hands to me expanded,
  His legs and his thighs to me likewise;
  And by my barbarous cruel entreatment
  This very next day this poor boy died.

5 I asked my men if they'd release (?) me
  If I'd give them golden store.
  Out of my cabin straightway they hauled me,
  A prisoner brought me on Bristol shore.

6 And now in Newdigate I am confined,
  The writ of death I do deserve;
  If I had been ruled by my servants
  This poor boy's life might have been preserved.

7 You captains all throughout this nation,
  Hear a voice and a warning take by me.

Take special care of your apprentice
While you are on the raging sea.

with my garling-spikk I misused him: with my gasket I did misuse him. A gasket
was a piece of rope, used to secure a sail.
Newdigate: Newgate

54   Ward the Pirate

'Here in Tunneis I met an English Captain, general Waird, once a great
pirate and commander at sea; who in despite of his denied acceptance in
England, had turned Turk and built there a fair palace, beautified with
rich marble and alabaster stones.' So wrote the Scots traveller, William
Lithgow, in 1616. John Ward was born at Faversham, Kent, and
worked as a fisherman. By 1601 he was living at Plymouth, where he
joined the navy. He soon turned pirate, made his way to the Mediterra-
nean, and became the commander of a pirate fleet with a combined crew
of 500 men. A single one of his prizes, a Venetian galeasse, was valued at
two million ducats. He died of the plague at Tunis in 1622, having
inspired, as John Masefield put it, 'a poetical play [*A Christian turn'd
Turke*, by Robert Osborne], two chap-books, a number of ballads, and
one knows not how many Royal Proclamations' (*A Sailor's Garland*,
1906, p.xvii). One might add the interest of naval historians, such as
Christopher Lloyd (*English Corsairs on the Barbary Coast*, 1981). 'The
Famous Sea-Fight between Captain Ward and the Rainbow', of which
the earliest extant copy dates from the late seventeenth century, was one
of the ballads. It was frequently reprinted, and survived substantially in
oral tradition for some 250 years. Compare Mr Carter's version, sung in
1905, with its opening verse: 'Strike up, you lusty gallants with musick
and sound of drum:/For we have descry'd a rover upon the sea is come;/
His name is Captain Ward, right well it doth appear/There has not been
such a rover found out this thousand year'. The balladeer's facts are
rather confused. Ward did open negotiations for a pardon (verse 3), and
offered James I, according to one report, 30,000 crowns; 'but even
James I jibbed at accepting bribes from such a notorious pirate and went
so far as to name Ward specifically in a proclamation of January, 1609,
for the apprehension of pirates' (Lloyd). As to the sea battle, 'there was a
ship called the *Rainbow* then in the navy, but she never fought with
Ward, nor did any other royal ship, so far as we can learn ... Perhaps

some merchantman named the *Rainbow* escaped from a running fight
with Ward, and perhaps her captain, or some man aboard her, made the
ballad in the glory of his heart' (Masefield). I should love to think so, but
it is more likely, alas, that some landlubber of a ballad writer took for
the name of a vessel that of Captain Rainsborow or Rainsborough, who
commanded the royal ship, *Samson*, in a successful action against
pirates off Malta in 1628. Rainsborough won further glory in 1637,
when he freed 300 captives from pirates at Sallee, in Morocco.

2 A ship was sailing from the east and going to the west,
   Loaded with silks and satins and velvets of the best;
   But meeting there with Captain Ward it proved hard to maintain:
   He robbèd them of all their wealth and bid them tell their king.

3 Captain Ward wrote a letter to our king on the fourteenth day of February,
   To know of him if he might come in and all his company,
   To know of him if he might come in old England to behold,
   And for his pardon he would give five hundred tons of gold.

4 O then the king provided a ship of noble fame,
   She's called the *Royal Rainbow*, perhaps you've heard her name.

[87]

She was as well provided for as any ship can be,
Full thirteen hundred men on board to bear her company.

5 O then this gallant *Rainbow* came crossing o'er the main,
   Saying: 'Yonder lies bold Captain Ward, and here we must remain'.
   'I'm here, I'm here'; cried Captain Ward, 'my name I'll not deny,
   But if you are one of the king's fine ships you are welcome to pass by'.

6 'O, no', says gallant *Rainbow*, 'it grieves our king full sore
   That his rich merchant ships can't pass as they have done before'.
   'Come on, come on', cries Captain Ward, 'I value you not a pin,
   For if you've got brass for an outward show, I've got steel within'.

7 O then the gallant *Rainbow* she fired, she fired in vain,
   Till six and thirty of their men all on the deck were slain.
   'Fight on, fight on', says Captain Ward, 'this sport well pleases me,
   For if you fight this month and more your master I shall be'.

8 It was eight o'clock in the morning when they began to fight,
   And so they did continue there till nine o'clock at night.
   'Go home, go home', says Captain Ward, 'and tell your king from me,
   If he reigns king all on the land, Ward will reign king in sea'.

55   Spurn Point

The vessel, *Industry* (Captain Burdon), was stranded on Spurn Point off
the mouth of the Humber on 4 January, 1868. Her captain declined the
proferred assistance of the lifeboat, and his ship became a total loss.
Vaughan Williams took down the tune and first verse in 1905 from an
ex-sailor, Mr Leatherday, in King's Lynn Workhouse, St James'
Hospital. The rest of the text has been added from broadside number 2,
issued by W. Forth, Waverley Street, Hull, under the title of 'Industry off
Spurn Point'.

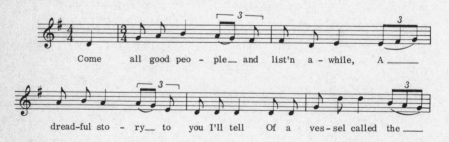

Come all good peo - ple__ and list'n a - while, A ____
dread-ful sto - ry__ to you I'll tell Of a ves - sel called the ____

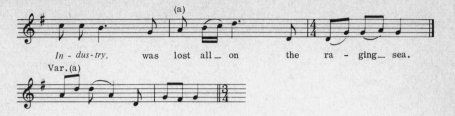

In - dus-try, was lost all _ on the ra - ging _ sea.

2 About seven o'clock on Sunday night
 She struck ground all on Spurn Point;
 The swelling waves ran mountains high;
 In a dismal state the ship did lay.

3 But when on shore we came to know,
 To their assistance we did go.
 We manned the lifeboat stout and brave,
 Expecting every man to save.

4 We hailed the captain who stood at stern:
 'We have come to save you and your men'.
 'We want no relief', he then did cry.
 'We shall get off at high water', he replied.

5 'Heave us a rope', we once more did say,
 'That alongside your ship we may lay'.
 'We want no relief', he then did cry.
 'I'd thank you to move off immediately'.

6 In the space of half an hour or more
 The lifeboat crew reached the shore.
 We watched her till eleven at night,
 Then in distress they hoisted a light.

7 Into the lifeboat once more we got
 And hastened to the fatal spot.
 Before we reached the fatal crew
 The light disappeared from our view.

8 O then we heard one poor man cry:
 'For God's sake, help me, or I shall die.
 My shipmates are gone, and so must I';
 And down he went immediately.

9 The captain was so obstinate;
 Into our lifeboat he would not get,
 Or else all hands we might have saved,
 And kept them from a watery grave.

[89]

John Reilly

The implacable opposition of a rich man to his daughter's match with a poor suitor leads to the death of both young people as they attempt to flee to America.

John Reil-ly is my true love's name;he lives down by the quay. He is as nice a young man as e-ver my eyes did see. My fa-ther he has ri - ches great, and Reil-ly he was poor; — Be - cause I loved my sai - lor dear he could not me en - dure.

2 My mother took me by the hand and these words to me did say:
   'If you are fond of Reilly you must leave this country,
   For your father says he'll take his life, and that without delay,
   So you must either go abroad or shun his company'.

3 'O mother dear don't be severe, where must I send my love?
   My very heart lies in his breast, as constant as a dove'.
   'O daughter dear I'm not severe, here is a thousand pound:
   Send Reilly to America to purchase there some ground'.

4 Now when she got the money to Reilly she did run,
   Saying, 'This very night to take your life my father charged his gun.
   Here is one thousand pounds in gold my mother sent to you:
   Sail off unto America and I will follow you'.

5 O when he got the money that night he sailed away,
   And when he got his foot on board these very words did say:
   'There is a token of your love, I break it into two.
   You have my hand and half my heart until I find her true'.
   ['You have my heart and half the ring until I find out you'].

6 About a twelve months after she came down to the quay;
  Young Reilly he came back again to take his love away.
  The ship got wrecked, all hands got lost, her father wept full sore;
  Young Reilly in his true love's arms lay drownded on the shore.

57   Young Henry the Poacher

It is my contention that this ballad first appeared in about 1830, perhaps in response to a number of well-publicised trials of poachers in the previous year or two. Many different printers issued versions, with some variation in the place names, but the norm seems to have been that the eponymous Henry was brought up in Warwickshire, lived near Southam, went poaching in Squire Dunhill's park, was tried at Warwick March Assizes, and sentenced to fourteen years' transportation. It is a matter of fact that at the Lent Assizes held at Warwick in 1829 eleven poachers were sentenced to death for shooting at the keepers of D. S. Dugdale, MP, on his estate near Atherstone. In May the sentences were commuted to transportation: for life in the case of five men and for fourteen years for the other six (the same number as in the song), whose names were David White, John White, William Goldby, James Mellor and *Henry* White (my italics).

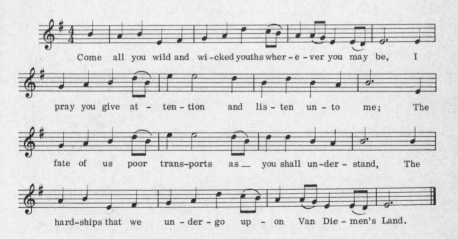

Come all you wild and wi-cked youths wher-e-ver you may be, I
pray you give at-ten-tion and lis-ten un-to me; The
fate of us poor trans-ports as you shall un-der-stand, The
hard-ships that we un-der-go up-on Van Die-men's Land.

2 My parents reared me tenderly, good learning gave to me,
  Till by bad company was beguiled, which proved my destiny.
  I was brought up in Warwickshire, near Southam town did dwell;
  My name it is young Henry, in Harbourn known full well.

3 Me and five more went out one night into Squire Dunhill's Park
To see if we could get some game, the night it provèd dark;
But to our great misfortune they trepanned us with speed,
And sent us off to Warwick Gaol, which made our hearts to bleed.

4 It was at the March Assizes to the bar we did repair,
Like Job we stood with patience to hear our sentence there;
There being some old offenders, which made our case go hard,
My sentence was for fourteen years, then I was sent on board.

5 The ship that bore us from the land, the *Speedwell* was her name,
For full five months and upwards, boys, we ploughed the raging main;
Neither land nor harbour could we see, believe it is no lie,
All round us one black water, boys, above us one blue sky.

6 I often looked behind me towards my native shore,
That cottage of contentment which we shall see no more;
Nor yet my own dear father who tore his hoary hair,
Likewise my tender mother, the womb that did me bear.

7 The fifteenth of September, 'twas then we made the land,
At four o'clock we went on shore all chainèd hand in hand;
To see our fellow sufferers we felt I can't tell how,
Some chained unto a harrow and others to a plough.

8 No shoes or stockings they had on, nor hat they had to wear,
But a leathern frock and linsey drawers, their feet and hands were bare;
They chained them up by two and two like horses in a team,
Their driver he stood over them with his Malacky cane.

9 Then I was marched to Sydney town without any more delay,
Where a gentleman he bought me, his book-keeper to be;
I took this occupation, my master liked me well,
My joys were out of measure, and I'm sure no one can tell.

10 We had a female servant, Rosanna was her name,
For fourteen years a convict was, from Wolverhampton came;
We often told our tales of love when we were blest at home,
But now we're rattling of our chains in foreign lands to roam.

Southam: small town near Warwick
Harbourn: (?) Harborne, then a
   village near Birmingham

Speedwell: there is no record of a
   convict transport of this name
Malacky: malacca
tell: count

Edward Jorgen

A man who appears to be of Scandinavian origin is arrested in Manchester and taken to Liverpool to stand trial on a charge of robbery. Somewhat improbably, he addresses his sweetheart from the dock. The song seems to be homemade, and to date from the nineteenth century. The words are slightly garbled, and perhaps incomplete. I have not seen any other version.

O Ed-ward Jor - gen is my name, and late-ly I to_
Eng-land came, To Man-ches-ter my friends to see, which
then did cause my des-ti-ny. On Mic-kles-moor Road I was
ta-ken near by po-lice-men, as_ you shall hear. I_
tried my pis - tol, my dag-ger drew, think-ing to_ run their bodies through.

2 The policemen there did boldly stand with all their truncheons in their hand,
And with me now they knocked me down, and laid me bleeding on the
    ground.
Captured I was and I went along to the New Buildings Prison strong;
To Liverpool was committed there, all for to take my trial there.

3 It's when my trial it does come on, before a judge I was forced to stand,
But never mind what they do say, they can but take my life away.
Now in the court this young man stand; his sweetheart came at his command.
Tears from her eyes in streams did flow when she heard of his overthrow.

4 He says: 'My dear, if I've done wrong, will you stay with me in prison
    strong?'
'Yes, that I will, while I have life. I wish I had been your wedded wife'.

'I have robbed many, dear heart, for greed, for which a great reward receive.
Out of his pocket this watch I drew. I robbed him of his money too'.

and lately: the MS reads at this point: *New Buildings Prison:* probably the
  'Degit (?)'   New Bailey Prison
Micklesmoor Road: ?

59   Just as the Tide was Flowing

To begin with, this song seems sweet, and even precious. The immaculate maiden sings a roundelay, the sailor makes a bow, the lambs skip
and play. Then it becomes frankly sexual, with the deeper meaning of
the recurrent phrase, 'just as the tide was flowing', very clear. Such open
sensuality has ensured that the song has seldom been printed in full,
while being a favourite with singers, especially sailors.

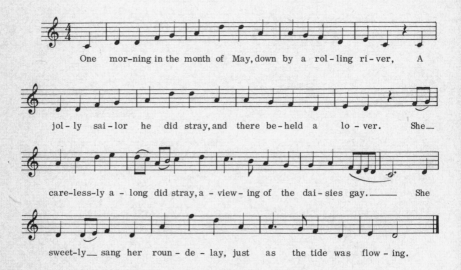

One mor-ning in the month of May, down by a rol-ling ri-ver, A
jol-ly sai-lor he did stray, and there be-held a lo-ver. She
care-less-ly a-long did stray, a-view-ing of the dai-sies gay.____ She
sweet-ly__ sang her roun-de-lay, just as the tide was flow-ing.

2 Her dress it was as white as milk, and jewels did adorn her skin:
  It was as soft as any silk, just like a lady of honour.
  Her cheeks were red, her eyes were brown, her hair in ringlets hanging down,
  Her lovely brow without a frown, just as the tide was flowing.

3 I made a bow and said: 'Fair maid, how came you here so early?
  My heart by you it is betrayed, and I could love you dearly.
  I am a sailor come from sea, if you'll accept my company
  To walk and see the fishes play, just as the tide is flowing'.

[94]

4 O it's there we walked and there we talked as we ganged down together;
   The little lambs did skip and play, and pleasant was the weather.
   O being weary we both sat down underneath a tree whose branches hung
      around,
   And what was done shall ne'er be known, just when the tide was flowing.

5 'O', she says, 'I've twenty pound in store. Meet me here when you will have
      more.
   My jolly sailor I adore all when the tide was flowing'.
   O it's to some public house we'll go where ale and wine and brandy flow.
   Success to the girl that will do just so, just as the tide was flowing.

60   The *Cumberland's* Crew

During the American Civil War – on 8 March, 1862, to be precise – a
Confederate frigate, the *Virginia*, which had the advantages both of
auxiliary steam power and iron cladding, sank two Federal vessels, both
wooden sailing ships: the frigate, *Congress*, and the sloop, *Cumberland*.
The latter was commemorated in a song which is still fairly well known
in North America, though it has seldom crossed the Atlantic. The singer
of our version was Mr Crist of King's Lynn, a seaman himself, who
might well have learned the song from an American shipmate. The
details in it remain fairly accurate, except that the sailors defending their
constitution against rebels have incongruously become British.

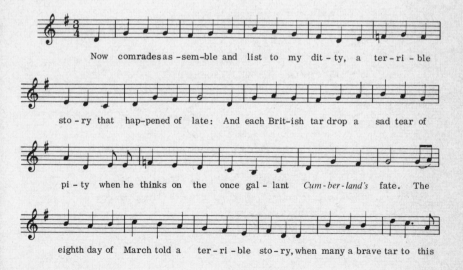

Now comrades as-sem-ble and list to my dit-ty, a ter-ri-ble
sto-ry that hap-pened of late: And each Brit-ish tar drop a sad tear of
pi-ty when he thinks on the once gal-lant *Cum-ber-land's* fate. The
eighth day of March told a ter-ri-ble sto-ry, when many a brave tar to this

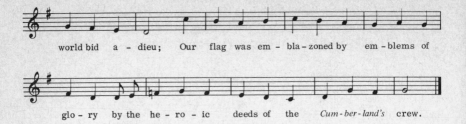

world bid a - dieu; Our flag was em - bla - zoned by em - blems of

glo - ry by the he - ro - ic deeds of the *Cum - ber - land's* crew.

2 On that fatal day about ten in the morning
   The sky it was clear and bright was the sun,
   When the drums of the *Cumberland* gave forth a warning,
   Which told every seaman to stand by his gun.
   An iron-clad frigate down on us came bearing;
   High in the air the rebel flag flew;
   The pennant of treason she proudly was wearing,
   Determined to conquer the *Cumberland's* crew.

3 Then up spoke our brave captain with stern resolution,
   Saying: 'Boys, of that monster we'll be not afraid.
   We have sworn to defend our beloved constitution,
   And to die for our flag, boys, we are not afraid.
   We will fight for our country because it is glorious,
   And to the old flag we'll ever prove true.
   We will die by our guns, boys, or conquer, victorious'.
   He was answered by cheers from the *Cumberland's* crew.

4 Now our noble ship's opened her guns' dreadful thunder;
   Our shot like hail on the rebels we poured.
   Our people gazed at her with awe-stricken wonder,
   As a shot struck her side and went harmlessly o'er.
   But the pride of our navy could never be daunted,
   Though the dead and the wounded our decks did bestrew;
   And the flag of old England still proudly we vaunted,
   Sustained by the pride of the *Cumberland's* crew.

5 Now broadside for broadside we poured down upon her,
   The blood from our scuppers ran down in dire gore;
   Our people gazed at her in awe-stricken wonder
   As a shot struck her side and went harmlessly o'er.
   She struck us amidships, our flanks she did sever,
   While her iron bows struck our noble ship through;
   And as slowly we sank in the dark rolling river,
   O still were the cheers of the *Cumberland's* crew.

6 Then slowly we sunk in Virginia's dark waters:
   We'll be honoured by the noble, the brave and the true.
   We'll be mourned by old England's brave sons and fair daughters,
   With the heroic men of the *Cumberland's* crew.
   We stood by our guns, boys, and never surrendered,
   And to the old flag, why, we ever proved true.
   With our flag proudly flying to our graves we went, dying,
   It was nailed to the mast of the *Cumberland's* crew.

many a brave tar: 'a bright tar' in the manuscript
the drums of the Cumberland: drums still beat to quarters in the American navy long after the practice was dropped by the British
brave captain: Lt George Morris
rolling river: the James River

61   The Loss of the *Ramillies*

Like sailors in general, Mr Crist seems to have been partial to songs of shipwreck and disaster. This song lasted for a century and a half, on both sides of the Atlantic, apparently without benefit of print. Conversely and perversely, 'The Fatal Ramillies', a different song on the same topic, while widely printed on broadsides in the nineteenth century, has turned up only once in oral circulation. The *Ramillies*, formerly the flagship of luckless Admiral Byng, was outward bound down the Channel in February 1760, when she encountered a series of fearsome gales. She started to leak, so turned back, but went a bay too far. As the *Gentleman's Magazine* put it: 'the unfortunate *Ramillies*, capt *Taylor*, with 734 men, being embay'd within the Bolt-head (which they had mistaken for the Ram-head, and imagined they were going into *Plymouth Sound*) and close up on the rocks, they let go their anchors, and cut away all their masts, and rode safe till five in the evening [of 15 February], when the gale increased so much 'tis impossible to describe; they parted, and only one midshipman [John Harrold] and twenty-five men out of the whole, jumped off the stern on the rocks, and were saved'. So much for a contemporary record, but the wreck of the *Ramillies* is still there in the cove which bears its name, and the villagers of nearby Inner Hope and Thurlestone still talk of the fatal night. There is one tradition that a local man on board the *Ramillies* tried to warn the officers of their error, but was put in irons for insubordination. The green at Thurlestone used to have a big depression where a mass grave had been dug, but this has now disappeared under the asphalt of a car

[97]

park. Some twenty years ago the skeletons of some *Ramillies* men were found under the dunes. They were collected by the council and taken to the rubbish tip.

O it hap - pened on a ___ cer - tain day, The ___
Ra - mil - lies to her an - chor she lay. The ___ ve - ry same night a ___
gale ___ came on, And a - way from her an - chor the good ship sprung.

Var. (a)

2 The rain it came down in a dreadful shock;
The seas they flew over our foretop.
With close-reefed topsails so neatly spread,
We were thinking to weather the old Ram's Head.

3 Our bosun cried: 'My brave fellows all,
Come list to me awhile for I can't find my call.
Now launch your boats your lives for to save,
For the seas this night they will surely be your grave'.

4 The boats they were manned and overboard were tossed;
Some they got in them but they were all lost.
Some went one way and some went another,
But the watch down below they all got smothered.

5 When the news unto pretty Plymouth came
That the *Ramillies* was lost with most of her men,
Pretty Plymouth's streets were flowing in tears
For the hearing of these sad, sad affairs.

6 Now all you pretty maidens whoever you may be
That lost your true loves in the bold *Ramillies*,
There was only two that was left to tell the tale
How the *Ramillies* went down in the January gale.

to her anchor she lay: 'she to her
   anchor lay' in the manuscript
Ram's Head: sailors' name for Rame

Head, to the west of Plymouth
Sound
call: whistle

62   John Raeburn

According to Robert Ford, who prints it under the title of 'Jamie Raeburn's Fareweel' (*Vagabond Songs and Ballads of Scotland*, 2 vols, Paisley, 1899–1901; vol. II, pp.55–6), this was 'a popular street song, all over Scotland, and sold readily in penny sheet form'. He claims that it was based on an actual incident, though without giving precise documentation: 'The hero of the verses ... was a baker to trade, who was sentenced to banishment for theft, more than sixty years ago'. The song is not often found in England, though it is sometimes sung to this day by travelling people.

2 My character soon taken was and I was sent to gaol.
   My friends stood all around me; there was none that could me bail.
   And then my old mother her grey old locks did tear,
   Saying: 'Son, O, son, what have you done to be sent so far awa'?'

3 When we reached the gangway leading to the ship,
  The guard stood all around me for fear I'd make a break.
  The guard stood all around me for fear I'd break awa',
  And try to regain the hills and dales of Caledonia.

4 There is a girl in Glasgow town, a girl I love so well,
  And if ever I do return again along with her I'll dwell.
  I'll quit all my night walking and shun bad company,
  And [bid] farewell to the hills and dales of Caledonia.

Son, O, son: 'O son' in the original   *night walking:* usually a euphemism
There is a girl: according to Ford, she   for poaching
    was called Catherine Chandlier

63   A Dream of Napoleon

Meeting Tom Paine in Paris, Napoleon told him that he slept with *The Rights of Man* under his pillow. Early in his career, Napoleon was admired by radicals, from Beethoven to the English and Irish Jacobins, who saw in him a possible liberator. Although this ballad seems to have been first printed in the late 1830s, it may have originated much earlier, and the only battle which it mentions took place in 1800. It is one of several about Napoleon and his family which were couched in high-flown language but nevertheless remained in oral circulation for upwards of a century. 'A Dream' is again from Mr Crist of King's Lynn; another Norfolk version, from the singer Sam Larner, can be heard on the record, *A Garland for Sam* (Topic 12T244, 1974).

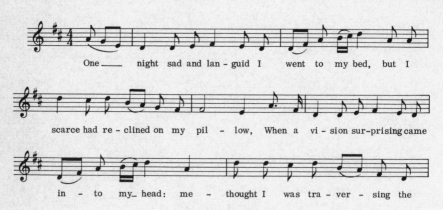

One___ night sad and lan-guid I went to my bed, but I

scarce had re-clined on my pil - low, When a vi - sion sur-prising came

in - to my_ head: me - thought I was tra - ver - sing the

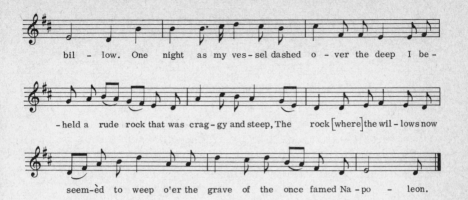

bil - low. One night as my ves-sel dashed o - ver the deep I be-
-held a rude rock that was crag-gy and steep, The rock [where] the wil - lows now
seem-èd to weep o'er the grave of the once famed Na - po - leon.

2 Methought that my vessel drew near to the land; I beheld clad in green this
    bold figure.
  With the trumpet of fame claspèd firm in his hand, on his brow there was
    valour and vigour.
  'O stranger', he cried, hast thou ventured to me from the land of thy fathers
    who boast they are free?
  If so a tale I'll tell unto thee concerning the once famed Napoleon.

3 'Remember that year so immortal', he cried, 'when I crossed the rude Alps
    famed in story
  With the legions of France, for her sons were my pride, and I led them to
    honour and glory.
  On the plains of Marengo I tyranny hurled and wherever my banner the eagle
    unfurled,
  'Twas the standard of freedom all over the world and the signal for fame',
    cried Napoleon.

4 'Like a soldier I've been in the heat and the cold, as I marched to the trumpet
    and cymbal,
  But by dark deeds of treachery I have been sold, while monarchs before me
    have trembled.
  Now rulers and princes their station demean, and like scorpions spit forth
    their venom and spleen,
  But liberty soon o'er the world shall be seen', as I woke from my dream, cried
    Napoleon.

Marengo: Italian village at which Napoleon defeated the Austrians in 1800

The Tarry Sailor

Two distinct songs share this title and the protagonists, Jack and Nancy. In one, which parallels 'The Green Bed' (no 12), a returning sailor pretends to be penniless, and is rejected by his sweetheart. When he produces 'handfuls of gold' she offers to marry him, but he in turn declines. In the other, opposition to a marriage comes from the father, but is overcome on production of 'bright gold'. This is the case in the version sung by Sally Brown of Ranworth, Norfolk. Her fragmentary text has been filled out from a broadside issued by Kendrew of York.

2 'O father, dear, do not us part, or strive to separate us,
For if you do 'twill break my heart; great grief it will create us.
His love to me is most sincere, and mine to him shall firm endure;
Betide me life or death, I'm sure I'll wed no other sailor'.

3 Up comes young Jack brisk as a bee, saying: 'My dearest Nancy,
  Now I am safe returned to thee, my heart's delight and fancy.
  I've been where stormy winds do blow, and oft have faced my deadly foe.
  Say, will you have me, aye or no, and wed poor Jack the sailor?'

4 'Two hundred pounds left by her aunt, three hundred more I'd give her;
  But if she marry without my consent a farthing I won't leave her.
  Besides, to marry she's too young, and sailors have a flattering tongue,
  So from my presence quick begone if you wed that tarry sailor'.

5 Says Jack: 'I don't regard that sum, my dear, I've gold in plenty.
  Believe me, sir, I do not come to court with pockets empty'.
  Five hundred guineas in bright gold upon the table there he told,
  And swept them into her apron fold: 'Take that, and Jack your sailor'.

6 Her father seeing his heart, that he behaved so clever,
  Said: ''Tis a pity you to part, and I'll not do it ever.
  As you so freely give your store, and you each other do adore,
  Now take her, Jack, here's as much more, for you are a clever sailor'.

7 Now messmates we've got safe to port, for I am sweetly married.
  I hope, my lads, we'll have some sport, and crown the day with claret.
  My frigate she is riggèd tight with silks and rings both gay and bright;
  I'll swear, my lads, to board tonight, and prove myself a sailor.

tarry: tarry was almost a generic adjective for sailors. The standing rigging on
  sailing ships was preserved with Stockholm tar, which adhered to the sailors'
  clothing
told: counted

65   Homeward Bound

'In sailing ship days this song was a prime favourite, and was sung all the
world over', wrote Captain W. B. Whall (*Sea Songs and Shanties*, 1910,
p.5). The name of the docks mentioned varies with the home port of the
vessel, but the *Dog and Bell* public house remains constant. This is one
of the very few shanties to have been printed on broadsides. Unusually,
too, for a shanty, this version was sung by a woman, Mrs Betty Howard.

(a)

1. Ou-r an-chor's weighed, our sails un-furled, We're bound to   cross the

CHORUS

wat'ry world. Don't you see we're homeward bound, Don't you see we're homeward bound?

Var. (a)

2. When you ar - rive at Li-ver-pool Docks You'll see the girls come

down in flocks. One to an-o-ther you'll hear them say: 'O

CHORUS

there comes Jack with nine months' pay'. Don't you see we're home-ward

bound, ____ Don't you see we're home-ward bound?

3 When we arrive at the *Dog and Bell*,
   The very best liquor they do sell;
   In comes the landlord with a smile,
   Saying: 'Drink, my lads, it's worth your while'.

4 Now your money is well nigh spent,
   There's none to be borrowed, none to be spent;
   In comes the landlord with a frown:
   'Get up, my lad, let Bill sit down'.

The third and fourth verses were sung to the same tune as the second.

66   Lovely on the Water

Lovers loath to part and exchanging tokens as a guarantee of fidelity:
the theme is well tried. Here, the man is going to sea as a volunteer,

[104]

having taken the bounty for the sake of his lover's 'aged parents'. The song, with its superlative tune, has been obtained only once from oral tradition. The words of the singer, Mr Hilton of South Walsham, Norfolk, have been completed from a broadside entitled 'Henry and Nancy, or the Lovers' Separation'.

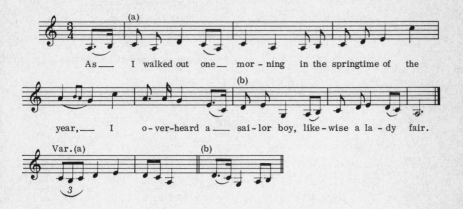

2 They sang a song together, made the valleys for to ring,
   While the birds on spray and the meadows gay, that proclaimed the lovely
      spring.

3 Said Henry to Nancy: 'We must soon sail away,
   For it's lovely on the water to hear the music play.

4 'For our queen she do want seamen, so I will not stay on shore.
   I will brave the wars for my country where the cannon loudly roar'.

5 'Oh', then said pretty Nancy, 'pray stay at home with me,
   Or let me go along with you to bear you company.

6 'I'll put on a pair of trousers and leave my native shore.
   Then let me go along with you where the cannon loudly roar'.

7 'It will not do', said Henry, 'it's in vain for you to try.
   They will not ship a female', young Henry did reply.

8 'Besides, your hands are delicate, and the ropes would make them sore;
   And it would be worse if you should fall where the cannon loudly roar'.

9 Poor Nancy fell and fainted, and soon they brought her to;
   They both shook hands together and took a fond adieu.

10 'Come, change your ring with me, my love, for we may meet once more.
   There's one above that will guard you, love, where the cannon loudly roar'.

[105]

11 'Four pounds is our bounty, and that would do for thee
   For to help thy aged parents while I am on the sea'.

12 For Tower Hill is crowded with mothers weeping sore,
   For their sons are gone to face the foe where the cannon loudly roar.

13 There's many a mother's darling has entered for the main,
   And in the dreadful battles what numbers will be slain.

14 For many a weeping mother and widow will deplore
   For those who fall by cannon balls where the cannon loudly roar.

67   The Holly Twig

To forestall a feminist furore, one should say that, although the song has
an unashamedly masculine viewpoint, its intention is not to advocate
taking a holly twig to one's wife. Its contribution to the battle of the
sexes is good-humoured and also allegorical. The song dates back to a
printed garland of about 1760 in which the benefits of bachelordom
listed include having a rapier with a Bilboa blade and also a silver-
spangled coat and waist-coat. According to Kidson it was sung by
Grimaldi in about 1820. More recent versions have been found on both
sides of the Atlantic.

When I was a ba-che-lor ear-ly and late I had a good trade as a lad can have. My gold and my sil-ver I let fly, And cocked up my leg and sang: 'Well done I!' Fol de lol day, fol de lol did-dle ay, Fol de lol did-dle ay, did-dle aye day.

[106]

2 On Monday morning I married a wife,
  Thinking to lead a sober life;
  I wished in my heart I had been dead
  Before I enjoyed her maidenhead.

3 So on Tuesday morning I went to the wood,
  Thinking to do my wife some good;
  I cut off a twig of holly so green,
  As fine a twig as ever was seen.

4 So on Wednesday morning I hung it to dry,
  And on Thursday morning I did it try:
  I laid on her back and I laid on her wig,
  Until I'd broken my holly twig.

5 On Friday morning to my surprise,
  A little before the sun did rise,
  She opened her mouth and begun to roar,
  And I thought in my heart she'd ne'er give o'er.

6 On Saturday morning she began her game;
  I beat her till she was blind and lame.
  The devil came in at the height of the game,
  And stole her away both blind and lame.

7 So on Sunday noon I dined [in state]
  Without a scolding wife or a howling mate;
  Now I'm enjoying my bottle and friend,
  And what do you think of my jolly week's end?

68   Bold Carter

Under the title of 'The Valiant Sailor', this first appeared in 1744 as one of 'three excellent New Songs' in 'The *Irish* Boy's GARLAND (EDINBURGH, Printed and Sold in *Swan-Close*, a little below the *Cross-Well*, *North-side* of the Street'). Through the long period of oral transmission since then the song has kept remarkably close to the same powerful text, and has usually been found with fine, soaring tunes. Vaughan Williams obtained this version from Mr J. Whitby, the sexton at Tilney All Saints, near King's Lynn.

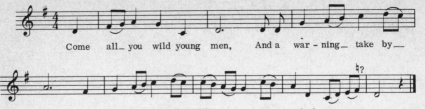

Come all you wild young men, And a war-ning take by me, And ne-ver lead your life a-stray Un-to bad com-pa-ny.

2 Bold Carter is my name,
   And hard is my intent;
   Till I got pressed by a press merchant,
   And on board a man of war got sent.

3 We hadn't sailed long
   Before the first thing that we spied,
   It was five French ships came sailing to war,
   And at length they were going to draw nigh.

4 We hoisted our main colours,
   Our bloody flag we let fly,
   Singing, every man stand to his gun,
   For the Lord knows the day he must die.

5 Our captain got wounded most wonderfully sore,
   And so did most of his men;
   Our whole ship's rigging got all shot away,
   So at last we were forced to give in.

6 Our decks were all sprinkled with blood,
   And the great guns so loud they did roar;
   I wished myself back home again
   With my Polly that I left upon the shore.

7 She's a tall [and a] handsome girl,
   She's a black [and] roving eye;
   And here upon the deck where I lay shot,
   For her sweet sake I must die.

8 Here's adieu to my father and my mother,
   Crying friends and relations, too.
   I never should have crossed the salt seas so wide
   If I had been ruled by you.

bloody flag: a red flag was hoisted as a signal for battle

[108]

Robert Bell describes this as a 'highwayman's song', dating probably from 'the age of Charles II' (*The English Poets*, 1857, p.218). However, in the version he prints the horse is used to escape from a highwayman ('Scampsman'), and the underworld cant employed has a raffish, Regency flavour. It concludes:

If any frisk or milling match should call me out of town,
I can pass the blades with white cockades, their whiskers hanging down;
With large jack-towels round their necks, they think they're first and
    fast,
But, with their gapers open wide, they find that they are last.

If threescore miles I am from home, I darkness never mind,
My friend is gone, and I am left, with pipe and pot behind;
Up comes some saucy kiddy, a scampsman on the hot,
But ere he pulls the trigger I am off just like a shot.

If Fortune e'er should fickle be, and wish to have again
That which she so freely gave, I'd give it without pain;
I would part with it most freely, and without the least remorse,
Only grant to me what God hath gave, my mistress and my horse.

A Mr Tuffs, Senior, sang our version to Vaughan Williams in 1911.

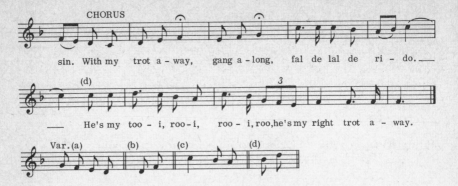

sin. With my trot a - way, gang a - long, fal de lal de ri - do.

(d) He's my too - i, roo - i, roo - i, roo, he's my right trot a - way.

Var. (a) (b) (c) (d)

2 He's an eye like a hawk, he's a nose like a swan,
   A foot like a cat, and his back you may span;
   He's rising four years old, all over right and sound,
   And if he makes a false step I'll lose a thousand pound.

3 If I'm twenty miles from home in the dark I'll never mind,
   With my pipe and my glass and my friends I'll leave behind.
   I'll clap the saddle on his back and away from them will ride:
   I'll pass them all upon the road and leave them far behind.

70   Liverpool Play

On 21 August, 15 September, 4 November (or unspecified date), a ship
called the *Dolphin, London, Lion, Delamore, Britannia* (or unspecified); lying in Liverpool Straits, Plymouth Sound, near Spithead, or,
amazingly, 'in the town of Nottingham'; under Captain Summerswell,
Foster (or unspecified); sails out and encounters a French ship or 'a ship
from Windsor' off the coast of Ireland or Africa, vanquishes it, and
brings it home as a prize. This song for all seasons, or rather for all
contingencies, has seldom been printed, but has travelled widely. It is an
expression of fierce, patriotic fervour, though there is a certain chill in
the orders to 'sink and destroy, my boys, wherever we do go'.

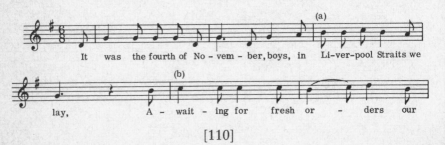

It was the fourth of No - vem - ber, boys, in Li - ver-pool Straits we
lay, A - wait - ing for fresh or - ders our

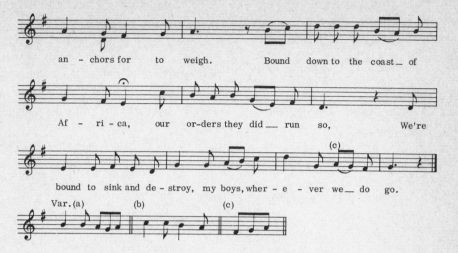

an - chors for to weigh. Bound down to the coast — of Af - ri - ca, our or-ders they did — run so, We're bound to sink and de - stroy, my boys, wher - e - ver we — do go.

Var. (a) (b) (c)

2 Now we had not been sailing scarce sixty leagues or more,
Before we spied a large French ship, and down on us she bore.
She hailed us in French colours to ask from whence we came.
'We've just come down from Liverpool town, and the *Dolphin* is our name.

3 'Are you a man of war, sir? Pray tell me what you be'.
'I am no man of war, sir, but a pirate you do see.
So heave up your fore and main yards, and let your ship come to,
For our tackles are hauled and our boats all lowered – or else we will sink
    you'.

4 Now our captain being an English man on the quarter-deck did say:
'Let every man stand true to his gun and we'll show them Liverpool play.
If it had not been for my own brother this battle would never've been tried;
Let every man stand true to his gun and we'll give to them a broadside'.

5 To broadside, to broadside, which caused all hands to wonder,
To see her French and lofty spars come rattling down like thunder.
We shot them from our quarter-deck till they could no longer stay;
Our guns being smart we played a good part, and we show them Liverpool
    play.

6 This large French ship was taken to Liverpool Docks and moored;
We fired shots at our sweethearts and fancy girls ashore.
We lowered down the French colours and let fly the red, white and blue;
We drunk success to the *Dolphin* and all her gallant crew.

[111]

The Man of Birmingham Town

A sailor returns from sea to find his wife not only spending his money freely, but cuckolding him (or 'cockling' him, as one version has it) into the bargain. He attempts to teach her a lesson by beating her with a rope's end. Nevertheless, like 'The Holly Twig' (no 67), the song is good-humoured in tone. It was popular in Norfolk, and the town of the title was probably one of the four Burnhams in the county. Versions of the song from elsewhere, including one from Nova Scotia, are called 'The Man of Dover'.

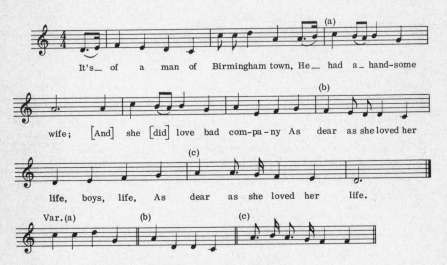

It's— of a man of Birmingham town, He— had a— hand-some wife; [And] she [did] love bad com-pa-ny As dear as she loved her life, boys, life, As dear as she loved her life.

Var. (a) (b) (c)

2 Now this poor man would go to sea
   His living for to get.
   Where he made one penny she spent two,
   It was all for the want of wit.

3 Now this poor man came home from sea,
   Being late all in one night,
   Enquiring for his own dear wife,
   His joy and his heart's delight.

4 O the servant girl made this reply
   With a voice so wonderful strong:
   'She's gone unto the neighbour's house.
   I think she will tarry long.

5 'O shall I go and fetch her home?'
   The poor man he began to think;

'No', says he, 'I will go myself,
And there I will choose to drink'.

6 Now as he was a-going along of the road
He heard such a wonderful noise.
Who should it be but his own dear wife,
Along with the Birmingham boys, brave boys.

7 'Go fetch another full bumping glass,
And I'll set on your knee;
And we will spend our money free
While our husbands are on the sea'.

8 This poor man he stood a-thinking;
His heart was nearly broke.
Then he went back and sent the maid,
While he prepared a rope.

9 Then she came jumping and skipping in,
Gave him such a joyful kiss;
Saying: 'You're welcome home, kind husband dear,
Long time you have been missed'.

10 He beat her once, he beat her twice,
Till she was wonderful sore;
And she cries out: 'O husband [dear],
I'll never do the likes any more'.

11 So come all you girls in Birmingham town,
A warning take by me;
And never spend your husband's money
While he is on the sea.

12 For if you do they'll make you rue,
And curse the hour you were born;
For cuckolding of your husbands dear,
They'll make you wear the horns.

72   Horse Race Song

There are similarities here with other horse racing songs, but this one seems to be unique. It no doubt commemorates a race held for a private wager, but documentation is lacking.

[113]

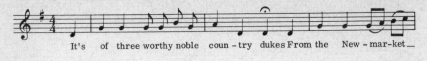

It's of three worthy noble coun-try dukes From the New-mar-ket

came. All for a—wa-ger they did run, And the ri-ders to do the

same, the same, And the ri-ders to do the same.

2 And as they were riding along the road
   They met with a little boy.
   'Come show to me Lord Framplin's halls,
   That his horses we may see'.

3 Then he took them into his middlemost stable,
   Amongst those riders all.
   There was 'Great Greasy Heel', 'Little Lampboy Jack',
   'Little Molly' shall run with you all.

4 Then up bespoke the poorest duke,
   The poorest of those three:
   'I'll run you for thirty thousand pounds,
   And tomorrow shall be the day'.

5 So when Lord Framplin heard those words,
   He stood with his hat in his hand:
   'I'll run you for gold whilst gold shall hold,
   And I'll make it upon your land'.

6 Then the drums and the trumpets we did sound,
   All for them to get ready;
   And all Lord Framplin had to say:
   'Mind you, Jack boy, and be steady'.

7 The first mile post they did come at,
   Lord Thompson's man did say:
   'If you can't go no faster than this,
   Kind sir, I'll show you the way'.

8 The second mile post they did come at,
   The people all declared
   They hardly could decide the case
   Between the horse and the mare.

9 There was heel to heel and toe to toe,
   So merrily they did run on;
   They were shoulder to shoulder and flank to flank,
   And the whip and touch began.

10 And just as they did climb the hill,
   Lord Framplin's mare being free,
   She took to her heels and away did run,
   And Lord Framplin he carried the day.

73   Bonny Robin

This is one of the songs of which Francis Place strongly disapproved: 'all
of them from ballads, bawled about the streets, and hung against the
walls. It will seem incredible that such songs should be allowed but it
was so. There is not one of them that I have not myself heard sung in the
streets, as well as at Chair Clubs, Cock & Hen Clubs & Free & Easy's'
(*Autobiography*, ed. Mary Thale, Cambridge, 1972, p.58). Its title was
Gee Ho Dobbin, and one of the milder verses ran: 'Her Breasts were as
soft and as white as New Cream,/And her motion kept Time with the
Bells of my Team;/When her Bubbies went up, her plump Buttocks went
down,/And the Wheels seem'd to stand, and the Waggon go round;/Ah
brave Roger, drive on Roger, ah brave Roger, hi ho'. 'Bonny Robin' is a
very rare, possibly unique, twentieth-century oral survival.

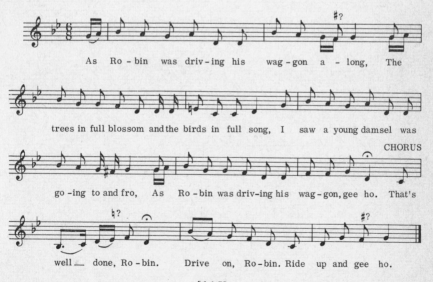

[115]

2 I hastened my horses to walk by her side;
   The roads being dirty I asked her to ride.
   I heaved her up gently, lay her at her ease;
   Then it's: 'Come and lie with me, young man, if you please'.

3 But if this young damsel should ask me my name,
   There's some call me Robin and some call me Ben;
   But as for the other one I dare not tell,
   For fear this young damsel should chance for to swell.

74 The Keys of My Heart

In another sexist skirmish a suitor tries to persuade a lady to accept his
hand in marriage by promising all sorts of gifts ranging, in different
versions, from greyhounds to gowns, from shoes to silver, and even
(thus giving a well-known title) the keys to Heaven – or Canterbury. My
personal favourite is 'a bed of down so soft/For you to lie under and I to
lie aloft'. There are two different *dénouements*. In one, when the auction
has reached its zenith the lady accepts, only for the man to turn the
tables by rejecting her ('When you might you would not;/Now you will
you shall not'). In the other, the lady accepts when the man offers the
key to his heart.

' O   ma-dam I pre-sent __ you a   fine coach and six   And
four black hor - ses as black as a - ny jet,   If   you   will walk a -
[pitch]
- broad with me,   If   you will walk a - broad with   me.'

2 'O I won't accept your fine coach and six,
   Four black horses as black as any pitch,
   Nor I won't walk abroad with you,
   Nor I won't walk abroad with you.'

3 'O madam, I present you a fine easy chair,
   To set in the garden and take the morning air,
   If you', *etc.*

4 'O I won't accept', *etc.*

5 'O madam, I present you a fine silken gown,
   Four yards long all a-trailed on the ground,
   If you', *etc.*

6 'O I won't', *etc.*

7 'O madam, I present you a fine gold watch
   To hang by your side to tell you what's the time,
   If you', *etc.*

8 'O I won't', *etc.*

9 'O madam, I present you the keys of my chest
   And all my gold, jewels, and jewels I possess,
   If you', *etc.*

10 'O I won't', *etc.*

11 'O madam, I present you the keys of my heart,
    And married we will be, and will never, never part,
    If you', *etc.*

12 'O I will accept the keys of your heart,
    And married we will be, and never, never part,
    And I will walk abroad with you,
    And I will walk abroad with you'.

75   Lullaby

Traditional lullabies are rare in English, though they still flourish in Gaelic-speaking parts of Britain and also in Europe. Oddly enough, the anti-soporific dandling song is much less uncommon in England. This lullaby came in 1906 from a Mr Thompson of Dunstan, Northumberland, who had learned it from his mother fifty years previously. It was still sung by the mothers of Dunstan to their children. I wonder if it still is.

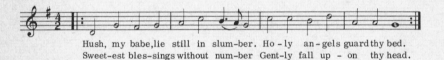

Hush, my babe, lie still in slum-ber. Ho - ly an-gels guard thy bed.
Sweet-est bles-sings without num-ber Gent-ly fall up - on thy head.

2 Hush, my babe, lie still in slumber.
Cold and hard thy saviour lay
When his birthplace was a stable,
And his softest bed was clay.

76   Willy Foster

Charley Warlie, Dolly Beardy, Katie Bairdie and Simon Brodie are among the different heroes of this little song, which, the Opies tell us, 'is more than three centuries old' (*Oxford Book of Nursery Rhymes*, 1977 ed., no 98). This variant was circulating by the mid-nineteenth century, and perhaps earlier.

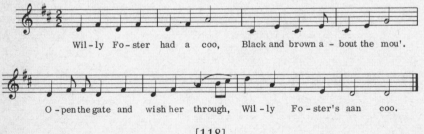

Wil-ly Fo-ster had a coo, Black and brown a - bout the mou'.

O-pen the gate and wish her through, Wil-ly Fo-ster's aan coo.

2 Willy Foster had a hen,
  Cockle but and cockle ben;
  She lays eggs for gentlemen,
  But none for Willy Foster.

3 Willy Foster's gyen to sea
  Wi' silver buckles on his knee.
  When he comes back he'll marry me,
  Canny Willy Foster.

77   Bizzoms

Songs from a female viewpoint are relatively uncommon, and a number of them express frank pleasure in sexuality. It is a vexed question whether this was a genuine expression of female opinion or a male counterfeit. Certainly, 'The Besom Maker' is usually found in the repertoire of male singers. Perhaps it expresses wishful thinking on their part; perhaps it is equally satisfying to both sexes. Vaughan Williams did not collect songs in Somerset, no doubt since the county was being intensively covered by his friend, Cecil Sharp; but the Mr Brice who sang this song came from Crewkerne, where he had learned it from an old fiddler called 'Blind Jimmy'.

I am a biz-zom ma-ker, the truth to you I'll tell. I am a biz-zom ma-ker, I live in yon-der dell. Plea-sure I do take, mor-ning, night and noon, Trip-ping o-ver the hills— and I ga-ther all sweet broom.———

CHORUS

Who'll buy my biz-zoms, biz-zoms fine and new? Come and buy my biz-zoms, bet-ter ne-ver grew.

2 As I walked over the hills, 'twas on a summer's day,
   I met a rakish squire, with a black and roving eye.
   He tips to me the wink and I gave to him the tune;
   I eased him of his jingle O, to gather all sweet broom.

3 As I walked out one night, 'twas from my native cot,
   I met Jack Sprat the miller, he was happy with his lot.
   His mill I rattled round, I ground his grits so clean;
   I eased him of his chink in gathering broom so green.

4 One day as I was turning to my native cot
   I met a buxom farmer, happy was his lot.
   He ploughed his furrow deep, he plant his seed so low;
   He left it in the soil young bizzoms for to grow.

5 When the corn grew up all in its native soil
   A pretty sweet young baby soon on me did smile.
   I packed up my bizzoms, I carried them to the fair,
   I sold my bizzoms of the best and spent the profit there.

Last chorus:

Bizzoms in the kitchen, bizzoms in the hall;
Bizzoms in the parlour among the ladies all.

broom: symbol of sexual love *I sold my bizzoms of the best . . . :* a
grits: millstones   broadside reads: 'I sold them all by
chink: money   wholesale, nursing's now my care'.

SUFFOLK

78   Eggleston Hall

With its evocative details and its main picture of frenetic gambling, this song gives a strong flavour of the world of the late eighteenth century and Regency. One of Vaughan Williams's singers who came from Essex called it 'Ingatestone Hall', and described it as 'a true song'. Although not apparently printed before 1907 it was widely popular, especially in the south of England, with the place of the horse-racing often being given as Epsom, and in one instance as Ipswich.

2 I took my coach and six pair horse the races for to see,
   'Twas here I spent ten thousand pound all in the light of one day.
   As I was turning home again the dibs they did run small:
   'Twas here I came a broken-down gentleman, and that's the worst of all.

3 And here my landlord seized my land, and bailiffs he sent three.
   He took away all I had got, and said he must take me.
   O then my family and wife all unto me did cry,
   To think that I should lie in gaol until the day I die.

dibs: money   *lie in gaol: sc.,* for debt

79   Wild and Wicked Youth

At a conservative estimate, between 1196 and 1783 some 50,000 people
were put to death at Tyburn (near to the present Marble Arch, in
London). A ladder was placed against the gallows, the prisoner mounted
with a rope round his neck; then the ladder was removed and he slowly
strangled. As Edward Thompson has written, 'the procession to Tyburn
(later, the scaffold outside Newgate) was a central ceremonial of
eighteenth-century London. The condemned in the carts – the men in
gaudy attire, the women in white, with baskets of flowers and oranges
which they threw to the crowds – the ballad-singers and hawkers, with
their "last speeches" (which were sold even before the victims had given
the sign of the dropped handkerchief to the hangman to do his work): all
the symbolism of "Tyburn Fair" was the ritual at the heart of London's
popular culture' (*The Making of the English Working Class*, 1963,
p.61). As well as last speeches there were last songs – called goodnight
ballads – and this one is archetypal. According to Frank Purslow it
originated in Ireland, where versions still often feature Newry Town and
St Stephen's Green, Dublin; but I have my doubts. In any event, its wide
diffusion in England is attested by a plethora of variants and titles:
'Flash lad', 'The Undaunted Youth', 'Adieu, adieu', and more. The
singer here was Robert Hurr. Vaughan Williams collected from two
others of the same family, William (for whom, see no 82) and also Ben
Hurr.

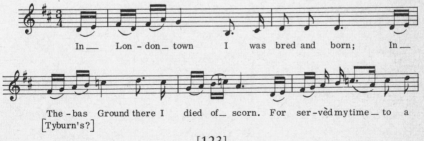

In — Lon - don — town   I   was bred and born;   In —

The - bas Ground there I   died of— scorn. For ser - ved my time — to   a
[Tyburn's?]

[123]

sad-dler's trade   I was   al - ways coun - ted but a   ro - ving blade.

2 For at seventeen I took a wife:
   I loved her dearly as I loved my life.
   For to maintain her both fine and gay
   I took up a robbing on the king's highway.

3 I robbed Lord Dukses I do declare,
   And lovely Nancy with the golden hair.
   We shuttered the shutters, bid them goodnight,
   And carried the gold to our heart's delight.

4 Then when I am dead let them carry me;
   Give them broadswords and sweet liberty.
   Let six blooming lassies bear my pall:
   Give them white gloves and pink ribbons all.

Lord Dukses: lords and dukes (?)

Most broadside versions continue thus after verse 3:

   Through Covent Garden I took my way
   With my pretty blowen to see the play,
   Till the Fielding's gang did me pursue:
   Taken I was by the cursed crew.

   But when I'm dead and carried to my grave,
   A pleasant funeral let me have.
   Six highwaymen to carry me:
   Give them broadswords and sweet liberty.

   Six blooming girls to bear up my pall:
   Give them white gloves and pink ribbons all.
   When I'm dead they may tell the truth:
   There goes a wild and undaunted youth.

[Or '*a wild and wicked youth*' – hence the title].

80   The *Royal George*

The lack of detail makes it impossible to be sure, but the song may refer
to the loss of the *Royal George* during the battle of Southwold Bay in

1673 (for which, see no 38), especially as it comes from a Southwold singer. If so, it is an amazing survival. Another *Royal George* was lost with 900 men in a spectacular accident at Spithead, in 1782.

As— we set sail from the Rock of Gib-ral-tar, ____ As [for] we set sail from sweet Dub-lin Bay, Oh lit-tle did we think of our sad mis-for-tune, ____ A - sleep-ing in the bri-ny sea. Oh— lit-tle did we think of our sad mis-for-tune, ____ ____ A - sleep-ing— in the bri-ny sea.

Var.(a) (b)
V.2&3 V.2 or

2 Oh there was one poor woman a-living in the city;
As soon as she heard that her husband was dead,
It filled her (?) poor heart with grief and pain
To hear what that poor woman said.

3 She said: 'I'll go and seek for my own true lover,
I'll go and sail the wide world round;
Then if my own true lover I do not discover,
All in some salt seas I will drown'.

81   Jack Tar

The epic sprees of Sailor Jack on shore with money to burn were the subject of many a song and story. In the days of prize money there were from time to time occasions such as that in 1762 when every seaman from two British frigates received £485 as his share from the capture of the Spanish treasure ship, *Hermione*. The most famous piece of extravagance which followed was the ceremonial frying of gold watches. Another boisterous celebration of prize money is depicted in Rowlandson's print, *Portsmouth Point* (1799). In perhaps a less dramatic way, such incidents went on throughout the age of sail (see for example Stan Hugill's *Sailortown*, 1967), and are even now not unknown. Moralists (and realists) did not hesitate to point out that Jack was welcome only as long as his money lasted, and some sailors' songs give similar warnings. This one, from an unnamed singer in Hadleigh Workhouse, is rare, turning up only very occasionally in England, and also in Nova Scotia.

Come all you roar-ing boys that de-light in sea-man's fare, Come lis-ten a-while to my song; For when Jack comes on shore with his gold and sil-ver store There's none can get rid of it so soon.

2 The first thing Jack demands is the fiddle in his hands
   And good liquor of every kind,
   With a pretty girl likewise with two dark and rolling eyes,
   And Jack Tar is suited to his mind.

3 The landlady she rolls in; when she finds him in good trim
   She appears like an evening star.
   She's ready to wait on him when she finds him in good trim,
   And she chalks him down two for one at the bar.

4 Now this game goes very well till Jack's money is all gone,
   When the old girl begins for to frown;
   With a nasty, glaring eye and a cat's string loosely tied,
   Saying: 'You, sailor, it is time you were gone'.

[126]

5 Now Jacky in a rage threw the candlestick at her head
And the glasses of every kind;
When the old girl in a fright called the watchmen of the night,
Saying: 'Take this jolly sailor to be gone'.

6 Now Jack he understands there's a ship in want of hands,
To the East Indies they are bound;
With a sweet and pleasant gale Jack unfolds the lofty sail,
And bids farewell to the girls of the town.

7 You may lay her on a tack like a cutter or a smack
As she rolls from the lee to the weather;
You may sail her in the wind's eye, that's as close as she will lie,
And I'm sure she'll afford you much pleasure.

cat's string: string from a cat o' nine tails (?)

82   Lovely Joan

A wily maid tricks a predatory man, depriving him both of his money
and his sexual gratification. The song is clearly a descendant (first
published in the nineteenth century) of 'The Baffled Knight' (Child 112;
see no 83). In the best known version, collected in Norfolk by Vaughan
Williams (see my *Everyman's Book of English Country Songs*, 1979, no
64), the male figure is merely 'a fine young man'; but here Mr William
Hurr of Southwold, Suffolk, specifically mentions a knight, as does the
broadside which has been used to supplement his fragmentary text.

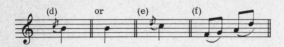

2 Then he pulled out a purse of gold,
   And said: 'Pretty maid all this behold.
   All this I'll give with me to wed'.
   Her cheeks they blushed like roses red.

3 'Now, noble knight, I pray you forbear,
   But don't you make remarks on me.
   Tomorrow morning I'm going to be wed,
   And my love shall enjoy my maidenhead'.

4 'Twas then he made a solemn vow,
   That he would wed, whether or no;
   This he said to frighten Joan,
   As she sat milking all alone.

5 'Give me the gold, sir, in my hand,
   And I will be at your command;
   For that will be more good to me
   Than twenty husbands, sir', said she.

6 Whilst he was looking for a bed,
   She mounted on her milk-white steed.
   He called, he called, 'twas all in vain;
   She never looked back [at him] again.

7 She did not think herself quite safe
   Until she reached her true love's gate;
   She robbed him of his steed and gold,
   And left him the empty purse to hold.

8 Now it pleased her lover to the heart
   To see how well she had played her part.
   'Tomorrow morning we'll be wed,
   And I will be the knight instead'.

'The Over Courteous Knight' (as one title puts it) has the opportunity to make love to a woman, but accepts her excuse for postponement, only to be taunted and spurned when the occasion has passed. In some Spanish, French and Portuguese analogues, she pretends to be the daughter of a leper; in Danish and German versions, she does not wish to spoil the man's cloak by laying it in the dew. The earliest English version, in Ravenscroft's *Deuteromelia* (1609), tells us that the knight 'could not find a privy place', and so agrees to wait till they get to 'her father's hall'. The hay field first appears in texts of the late seventeenth century, and the dew on the grass in *Pills to Purge Melancholy* (1719). The song has a long pedigree, and is a splendid piece of feminine *hauteur*. The singer of this version was Mr Jake Willis, a veteran of the Crimean War and the Indian Mutiny.

2 I boldly steppèd up to her
And asked to lay her down, sir.
The answer that she gave me:
'The dew is on the ground, sir.

3 'Wait till you get to my father's house,
Where you may lay me down, sir;
Where you can have my maidenhead
All on a bed of down, sir'.

4 O when she got to her father's hall
That was walled in all round, sir,

She stepped in and shut the door,
And shut the young man out, sir.

5 'When you met with me at first
You did not meet a fool, sir;
You may take your Bible under your arm
And go a little more to school, sir.

6 'And when you meet a pretty maid,
Little below the town, sir,
You must not mind her squalling,
Nor the rumpling of her gown, sir.

7 'There is a cock in my father's yard,
He will not tread the hen, sir;
And I do think in my very heart
That you are one of them, sir.

8 'There is a flower in my father's garden,
It is called a marigold, sir;
An if you will not when you may
You shall not when you will, sir'.

marigold: is she accusing him of effeminacy?

84   The Basket of Eggs

A theme which seems to have fascinated ballad writers, for it occurs in a
good many different guises, is that of a man tricked into paying the
woman he has deserted, for the child he has fathered. In some versions
the couple part with acrimony after the money is paid, but here a
conventional coda involves wedding bells. This is not found in the
earliest printed version, published in 1796 under the title of 'Eggs and
Bacon' in *The Man of War's Garland*. The song was enormously
popular with country singers, and Vaughan Williams alone collected
several different versions.

There were two sai - lors set out a - walk - ing, Their

pock-ets be - ing both lined with gold; As they were walk-ing and

fond - ly talk - ing A — love-ly dam-sel they did be - hold.

2 With a great big basket standing beside her,
   She being weary sat down to rest.
   I kindly asked her if I should carry it,
   And the answer that she gave: 'If you please.

3 'Sailors, sailors, I know nothing of you:
   There's eggs in the basket, pray take care.
   If you should chance to overwalk me,
   At the half way house, pray leave them there'.

4 At the half way house they passèd by,
   And another alehouse they did draw nigh.
   'Landlord, landlord, bring out some bacon:
   There's eggs in the basket, we'll have a fry'.

5 The landlord went unto the basket,
   Thinking some eggs there to find:
   'Oh, jolly sailors, you are mistaken;
   Instead of eggs there is a child'.

6 One of the sailors set out a-fretting;
   The other one says: 'Not worth a while.
   Here's one hundred pounds I will pay down
   To any young woman that will take this child'.

7 Pretty Nancy standing by the fire,
   She hears the words the sailor said:
   'I'll take the child and kindly use it
   As soon as the money is paid down'.

8 'Are you the girl they call pretty Nancy,
   That I danced with last Easter Day?'
   'Oh, yes, kind sir, I took your fancy,
   And now the fiddler you must pay'.

9 'Let us go down to yonder chapel,
   And there the knot it shall be tied'.
   Bells are ringing, sailors singing;
   We will enjoy that happy bride.

[131]

At the end of the eighteenth century, when most men wore knee-breeches, sailors (apart from officers) wore trousers, and had been doing so for some fifty years. (Incidentally, the revolutionary French *sans-culottes* were so called, not because they went about with bare posteriors, but because they, too, wore trousers in preference to breeches). A sailor could easily roll up his wide trousers when decks had to be scrubbed, or seas were breaking over them. The trousers (usually spelled 'trowsers' at the time) were often stained with the Stockholm tar used on the standing rigging, and 'tarry trousers' were thus the unmistakable badge of the sailor. The song of the same name was a triumphant expression of a girl's preference for a sailor. It was later adapted to favour a soldier.

2 'Daughter, daughter, I would have you marry,
    No longer lead a single life'.
    'Oh, no', said she, 'I'd rather tarry
    For my jolly soldier bright.

3 'Mother, would you have me wed a farmer?
    Not to give me my heart's delight.
    Give to me the lad whose broad-striped trousers
    Shine to my eyes like diamonds bright.

4 'Soldiers they are lads of honour,
    They will face their enemies;
    Where the thundering cannons loudly rattle,
    And the bullets swiftly fly'.

[132]

Two classic songs, 'The Seeds of Love' and 'The Sprig of Thyme', deal with a woman's seduction and abandonment, largely through the symbolism of plants. They have tended to hybridise, and become almost indistinguishable, but they were originally separate, the first being from a masculine viewpoint, the second (of which 'The Red Running Rue' is a version) from a feminine angle. This has been contested, but the evidence of the first printed version seems clear: 'The Maid's Lament for the Loss of her Maiden-head' appeared in *Four Excellent Songs* (1766), 'Printed and Sold by William Forrest at the head of the *Cow-gate*' (Edinburgh). Even this is not the earliest version of all, for it clearly comes from oral sources, with garbling in places, possibly by the person who wrote it down. For example, 'The spink revileth the primrose' should be 'The pink, the violet and the primrose'; and 'wet full June', 'wait for June'. Vaughan Williams took down only the first and last verses, though, from his title, the singer must have known more of the song. I have supplied the rest of the words from an unidentified text in the composer's *Folk Songs of the Four Seasons* (1949, no 2). Thyme, known as the uterine herb, stands for the womb, and by implication, virginity; by a pun it also indicates time, and the chronological progression of the blooming of the flowers listed parallels the delay caused by the woman's indecision. The first three flowers symbolise purity: the primrose is tender; the pink, with its blush colour, is modest; the lily – associated with the Madonna, and known in parts of England as the May lily (both the month and the maid) – is virginal. These are replaced by the passion of the red rose, which in turn is succeeded by the regret of the rue and the bitter grief of the willow. All this is done with economy and directness, and the poignancy is all the stronger for the unrequited longing expressed in the last couplet.

[133]

2 My garden was planted full
 Of flowers everywhere;
 But for myself I would not choose
 The flower I held so dear.

3 The primrose I did refuse
 Because it came too soon;
 The lily and pink I overlooked,
 And vowed I would wait till June.

4 In June came the rose so red,
 And that's the flower for me;
 But when I gathered the rose so dear
 I gained but the willow tree.

5 My garden is now run wild.
 When shall I plant it new?
 And my bed that was once filled with thyme
 Is all overrun with rue.

6 Green willow it will twist,
 Green willow it will twine;
 And I wish I was in that young man's arms
 That once had this heart of mine.

87   The Barley Straw

A ballad in the collection of Samuel Pepys, 'The Pollitick Begger-Man',
relates how the maid at a farmhouse gives shelter for the night to a
beggar, who promises marriage, seduces her, then decamps, leaving her,
to her considerable annoyance, pregnant: 'Then she did take her milk-
pail,/and flung it over the wall:/'O the Devil go with my milk-pail,/my
maidenhead and all'. In what I take to be a later development the beggar
turns out to be a nobleman in disguise. One tradition has even identified
him as James V of Scotland, but Child tartly says that it 'has no more
plausibility than it has authority'. In the latter part of the eighteenth
century a new *rifacimento* appeared in song garlands as 'The Jovial
Tinker and Farmer's Daughter', or simply as 'The Jovial Tinker'. Here,
it is made clear from the outset that a nobleman wishes to 'gain the
maidenhead' of a farmer's daughter. He disguises himself as a travelling
tinker, and is lodged in the barn. When the farmer's daughter goes to
make his bed he takes the opportunity to lay 'her down upon the floor

among the pease straw'. Before departing he gives her fifty guineas, and tells her that his name is David Faw. In due course, she gives this name to the child, and her father offers a farm, cattle and money to a farmer's son to marry the 'damsel'. All three varieties were widely popular until recent years. Vaughan Williams's 'tinker' version came from an unspecified singer at Southwold, Suffolk. Verses 5 to 8 have been added from a garland text.

It's of a rich old far-mer___ who lived in Der-by-shire. He had one on-ly daugh-ter,___ most beau-ti-ful and fair. He had one on-ly daugh-ter,___ rich, hand-some, kind and free, And it's ma-ny a weal-thy far-mer's son would have gained her com-pa-ny.

2 It's of a rich young squire who lived there close by.
   He swore he would not be easy until he had a try,
   So he dressed himself as a tinker and travelled all on his way
   Till at last he came to the old farmhouse, and these are the words he did say.

3 'Bring out your pots and kettles, and any old tins to mend;
   Or have you any lodgings for me, a single young man?'
   'Oh, yes', replied this pretty maid, not thinking any harm,
   'You're welcome to stay here all night if you stay in my father's barn'.

4 Then supper being over she went out to make his bed.
   He quickly followed after her and stole her maidenhead.
   She, being brisk and lively, jumped up and barred the door,
   And she slept all night in her tinker's arms among the barley straw.

5 Oh, how the lassie blushed, and how she thought for shame:
   'Since you have got your will of me, pray tell to me your name'.
   He whispered softly in her ear, said: 'They call me David Faw;
   And if I chance to come this way again you'll remember the barley straw'.

6 Early the next morning before the break of day
   The tinker he put on his clothes and says: 'I must away'.
   He gave her fifty guineas, well tied up in a purse;
   He said: 'My dear, take your rest. I hope you're none the worse'.

7 When seven months were past and gone this maid looked white and wan,
   Then for to suspect her mother she began,
   Saying: 'Tell to me, my dearest, who've done to you this harm'.
   'I fear, this windy tinker that laid all in the barn'.

8 When nine months they were past and gone this fair maid had a son,
   And such a gossiping there was, likewise much mirth and fun;
   When the child he was baptised, they called him David Faw.
   That bonny lad was got that night among the barley straw.

88   The Lads of Kilkenny

The words of this song have been attributed to Thomas Moore (1779–1852), the friend of Byron and Shelley, who spent two years at Kilkenny in connection with the theatre there. However, Lucy Broadwood has suggested that the Irish composer, Michael Kelly (1762–1826), was responsible for both tune and words, which were adapted from traditional sources. Either way, the song was widely sung, not only in Ireland, but in England, where it is sometimes known as 'The Chaps of Cocaigny'. Vaughan Williams's singer pronounced the town as 'Kil-kainy'.

It's the boys ⎯ of Kil - ken - ny are stout ro - ving blades, And if e - ver they meet with some nice ⎯ lit - tle maids, They'll kiss and they'll court them and will spend their mo-ney free; And it's down in old ⎯ Ir - e - land Kil - ken - ny for me.

2 In the town of Kilkenny there runs a clear stream;
   In the town of Kilkenny there lives a fair dame.
   Her lips are like roses, her mouth much the same,
   Like a dish of fresh strawberries smothered in cream.

3 Her eyes are as black as Kilkenny's large coal,
   Which through my poor bosom has burnt a large hole.
   Her mind like its river is mild, clear and pure,
   But her heart is more hard than its marble, I'm sure.

4 Kilkenny's a pretty town and shines where it stands,
   And the more I think of it the more my heart warms.
   If I was at Kilkenny I should think myself at home,
   For there I got sweethearts but here I can get none.

5 I'll build my love a castle on Kilkenny's free ground:
   Neither lords, dukes nor squires shall ever pull down;
   And if anyone should ask you to tell him my name,
   I am an Irish exile and from Kilkenny I came.

89   The Ranter Parson

The term 'ranter' was applied to a sect of Primitive Methodists which originated between about 1807 and 1810. The song appeared several times on street ballads, but to the best of my knowledge has turned up only once in oral tradition: in 1904, when Vaughan Williams took it down from a 61-year-old labourer, who had learned 'most of his songs off "ballets" or from his father'. The tune is better known as 'The Rant'.

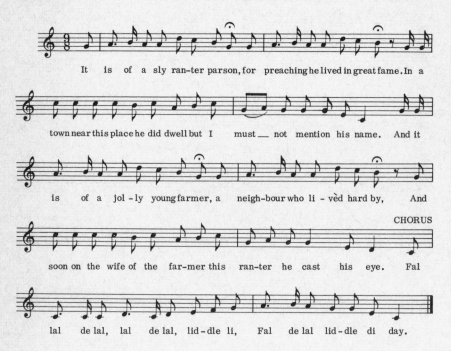

It is of a sly ran-ter parson, for preaching he lived in great fame. In a
town near this place he did dwell but I must not mention his name. And it
is of a jol-ly young farmer, a neigh-bour who li-vèd hard by, And
soon on the wife of the far-mer this ran-ter he cast his eye. Fal
lal de lal, lal de lal, lid-dle li, Fal de lal lid-dle di day.

2 While the farmer his work did mind, and rose with the lark in the morn,
  The ranter was forming a plan how to crown the farmer with horns;
  He oft to the farmer did go, and preach for the good of his soul,
  But when you hear of the joke I'll warrant you'll say it was droll.

3 Had you but the ranter seen you'd have thought him free of all evil,
  But though pure as snow-drift without, within was as black as the devil.
  One day as the farmer went out, thought he, I shall gain my desire,
  So unto the house he did start, and sat himself down by the fire.

4 He says: 'My dear lady, I'm told your husband won't be here tonight.
  I value not silver nor gold if I can but enjoy my delight'.
  'O then', she replied, with a smile, 'my husband is gone for a week'.
  The ranter he little did think how she meant to play him a trick.

5 The lady she laughed in her sleeve, and modestly hung down her head.
  She said: 'While my husband is out you are welcome to part of my bed'.
  The ranter was pleased to the heart, to think that he soon would be blest
  By crowning the farmer with horns; but now comes the cream of the jest.

6 When all things were silent at night she whispered these words in his ear:
  'The best bed it stands in the parlour, and you must go to it, my dear;
  And when you have got safe to bed, I'll come to you with all speed'.
  'All right,' said the ranter, 'make haste, and the bargain's agreed'.

7 The ranter he jumped into bed, and there lay snug as you please;
  The lady slipped into her garden and fetched in a hive of bees.
  She carried them into the parlour and threw them on the floor,
  And nimbly ran out and locked on the ranter the door.

8 The bees began buzzing about, the ranter he jumped on the floor:
  So neatly he capered and danced, while they stung him behind and before.
  At length he got out of the window, since no other way could he find;
  His clothes he ne'er stopped to take, but was glad to leave them behind.

9 All smarting and sore with stings he ran home to his wife in his shirt,
  Such a figure of fun for to see, all besmeared with mud and with dirt.
  Next morning the farmer came home; as I for a truth have been told,
  In one of the ranter's side pockets he found thirty bright guineas in gold.

10 The ranter he got in disgrace, the farmer he laughed at the joke,
  To think how the ranter would look without breeches, waistcoat or coat.
  The ranter he frets and he pines to think on the loss of his money;
  And the farmer, though he lost his bees, thinks he's well paid for the honey.

Two separate songs go under this title. The better known one normally begins; 'O Polly dear, O Polly, the rout is now begun'. The other, of which a version is given here, is otherwise known as 'The True Lovers; or, The King's (or Queen's) Command'. Both probably date from the Seven Years' War, during which a number of campaigns were fought in western Germany. The suggestion that women should be taken to the wars with their menfolk may now seem strange, but in fact a number of soldiers' wives were allowed to accompany armies, and they acted as cooks, laundresses and nurses. Vaughan Williams's singer was a 71-year-old shepherd, Mr Flint, who originally came from West Grinstead in Sussex. He was living at Lyne in Surrey when Vaughan Williams met him, in 1908, and there is no indication of where he learned his songs.

2 'That was not what you promised me when by you I was beguiled;
   You promised that you would marry me when you got me by [with] child.
   Oh, it's do not me forsake, and pity on me take, for great is my woe;
   Through France, Spain and bonny Ireland along with you I will go'.

3 'Those long-day weary travellings they will hurt your tender feet;
   Those hills and lofty mountains they will cause you for to weep.
   Besides, you would not like to yield and lay in the open field with me all night
       long;
   Your parents would be angry if with me you'd been along'.

4 'My parents I do not vally, my foes I do not fear;
   Along with my valiant soldier I'll travel both far and near.
   It's gold shall never me deceive or any other fee. Along with you I'll go
   To fight the French and Spaniards or any other daring foe'.

5 'Now you have been so venturesome and to venture your sweet life,
   The first thing I'll marry you and make you my lawful wife;
   And if anyone offend you it's I will defend them [you], and soon you shall see,
   And you'll hear the drums and trumpets sound in the wars of High
       Germany'.

vally: value

91   The Sailor Boy

'A Sailor's Life', 'The Sailing Trade', 'Sweet William': these are some of
the many titles of this well-loved song, which was known all over Britain
and North America. Its origin may lie in the wars between Britain and
France (1793–1815); certainly, one version says: 'Your true love,
William, is not here,/For he is killed and so I fear;/For the other day as
we passed by,/We seed him last in the *Victory*.'

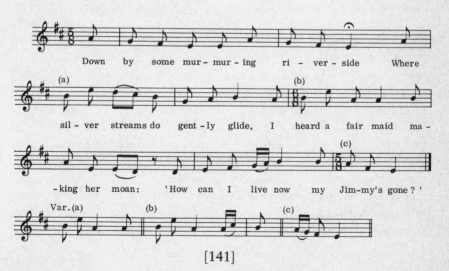

[141]

2 'O father, fetch me a little boat,
   That on the ocean I might float;
   And every ship I do sail by
   I will enquire for my sailor boy.

3 She had not sailed long in the deep
   Before some queen's ship she chanced to meet.
   'Come, jo'ful sailors, come tell me true
   If my young Jimmy sails along with you'.

4 'O no, fair lady, he is not here,
   For he is drownded; I greatly fear
   That yonders island we sailed by,
   It was there we lost your Jimmy boy'.

5 She wrung her hands, she tore her hair,
   Much like some woman in despair.
   Her boat up against some rock will run:
   'How can I live now my Jimmy's gone?

6 'I will go down to some shady grove;
   There I'll go and make my woe [moan],
   Telling the small birds, telling my grief,
   That they might grant me some such relief'.

92   Horn Fair

There was once a proverb, 'All's fair at Horn Fair', which reflected the
extremely relaxed nature of the proceedings at the fair annually held on
18 October at Charlton, Kent. Grose says: 'It consists of a riotous mob,
who after a printed summons dispersed through the adjacent towns,
meet at Cuckold's Point, near Deptford, and march from thence in
procession, through that town and Greenwich, to Charlton, with horns
of different kinds upon their heads.... The vulgar tradition gives the
following history of the origin of this fair: King John, or some other of
our ancient kings, being at the palace of Eltham, in this neighbourhood,
and having been out a hunting one day, rambled from his company to
this place, then a mean hamlet; when entering a cottage to inquire his
way, he was struck with the beauty of the mistress, whom he found
alone; and having prevailed over her modesty, the husband returning
suddenly, surprised them together; and threatening to kill them both,
the king was obliged to discover himself, and to compound for his safety

by a purse of gold, and a grant of the land from this place to Cuckold's Point, besides making the husband master of the hamlet. It is added that, in memory of this grant, and the occasion of it, this fair was established, for the sale of horns, and all sorts of goods made with that material' (*Dictionary of the Vulgar Tongue*, 1811 edition). The fair was suppressed in 1874, but has recently been revived.

As I___ was a - walk - ing one morn - ing in spring, So soft___ blew the winds and the leaves grow - ing green, I met a pret - ty dam - sel [all] on a grey mare, As she___ was a - ri - ding on to Horn___ Fair.

2 I asked this pretty damsel for to let me ride.
'O no'; then: 'O no, my mammy would sigh;
And besides my old daddy would bid me for sure,
And never let me ride on the grey mare any more.

3 'I can find by your talk you're for one game of play,
But you will not ride me nor my grey mare today.
You will rumple my muslin and uncurl my hair,
And I shouldn't be fit to be seen when I get to Horn Fair'.

4 'O, O my pretty damsel, how can you say so,
Since it is my intention Horn Fair to go?
We will join the best of company when we do get there,
With horns on our heads as fine as our hair'.

5 There were the finest of horns as ever you did behold,
There were the finest horns as were gilded with gold;
And ride merry, merry, merrily Horn Fair we did go,
Like jolly, brisk couples, boys, and all in a row.

This encounter between a soldier (sometimes a grenadier, sometimes a dragoon) and a lady is depicted with lazy sensuality. The tune came from a 60-year-old labourer who originated in Sussex. The text which has been added was taken down by Vaughan Williams from an unidentified singer.

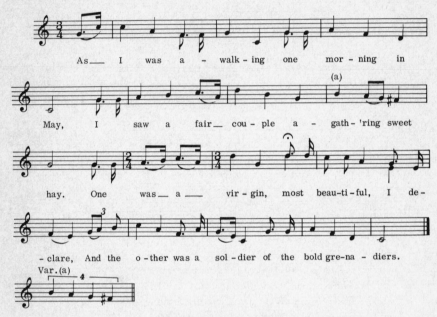

As— I was a - walk-ing one mor-ning in May, I saw a fair— cou-ple a - gath-'ring sweet hay. One was— a — vir-gin, most beau-ti-ful, I de--clare, And the o-ther was a sol-dier of the bold gre-na-diers.

Var.(a)

2 Then he claspèd one arm round her neck and one round her middle,
  And it's out of his knapsack he drew a long fiddle.
  O the tunes that he played, my boys, by the touching of the string,
  It's better see the flowers grow than hear the nightingale sing.

3 'O now', said the fair maid, 'It's time to give o'er'.
  'O no', said the soldier, 'let's have one or two chords more.
  In the liking of your music and the touching of the string,
  It's better to see the flowers grow than hear the nightingale sing'.

4 'O it's now', said the fair maid, 'will you marry me?'
  'O no', said the soldier, 'that never can be,
  For I've got a wife in my own country;
  She's the cleverest little woman my two eyes ever seen'.

After the hellfire sermon, the hellfire song – probably deriving from the climate of feeling produced by the religious revival of about 1816, which in turn harked back to the terrors of medieval apocalyptic imagery. The tune is now perhaps too familiar, for Vaughan Williams set it to the words of 'O Little Town of Bethlehem' (*The English Hymnal*, 1906). It is here restored to its own words, but those who find the association with 'O Little Town' impossible to shake off might prefer to use an alternative. Vaughan Williams obtained the song from a Mr Garman, who told him that he had previously sung it for the Rev. John Broadwood, 'who would always give half-a-crown to hear "The Ploughboy's Dream".' Broadwood was the editor of the first collection of English folk songs with their tunes: *Old English Songs, as ... sung by the Peasantry of the Weald of Surrey and Sussex* (1843).

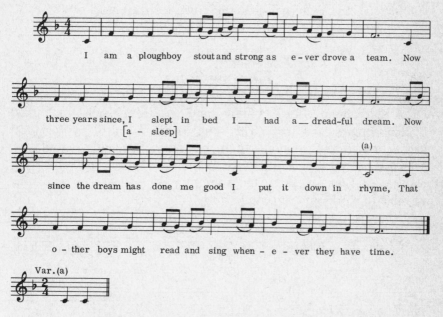

2 I dreamt I drove my master's team with Dobbin, Bald and Star,
   Before a stiff and handy plough, as all my master's are.
   I found the ground was baked so hard, 'twas more like bricks than clay;
   I could not cut my furrow through, nor would my beasts obey.

3 Now Dobbin lay down, both Bald and Star they kicked and snorted sore;
   The more I lashed and cursed and swore, the less my cattle stir.

[145]

Then, lo, above me a bright youth did seem to hang in air,
With purple wings and golden hands, as angels painted are.

4 'Give over, cruel wretch', he cried, 'nor thus thy beasts abuse.
Think, if the ground was not as hard, would they their work refuse?
Besides, I heard thee curse and swear, as if dumb beasts could know
What all thy oaths and curses meant, or better for them go.

5 'But though they know not there is one who knows thy sins full well,
And what shall be thine after doom another shall thee tell'.
No more he said, but, light as air, he vanished from my sight;
And with him went the sun's bright beams, and all was dark as night.

6 The thunder roared from under ground, the earth did seem to gape;
Blue flames broke forth, and in those flames, a dire, gigantic shape.
'Soon shall I call thee mine', it cried, with voice so drear and deep
That, quivering like an aspen leaf, I wakened from my sleep.

read and sing: an indication that the song originated as a printed ballad

95   Hunting Song

Dido, Ruler, Bonny Lass and Julius are the names of beagles, and 'puss'
is their quarry, the hare. The song seems to have been a local
production, to commemorate a particular hunt, though it may well have
been adapted from an earlier piece. 'Stringdoms' in the first verse is the
name of a field, so, given the appropriate knowledge, it would be
possible to work out a precise location.

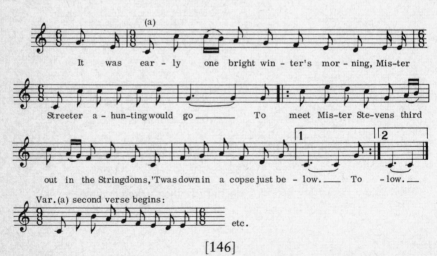

[146]

2 Dido began for to whisper,
   And presently she gave tongue;
   They holloa to covert and soon they did move her,
   So merrily they run her along.

3 They run her through rings and coverts
   And so fast as our dogs could give tongue
   Puss found it won't answer for the hounds follow faster,
   So out of the covert she run.

4 O she run by the *Three Jolly Sailors*,
   Rap'ly back fields she skipped;
   And prancing run by great Jack Francis,
   And then they were all at a stand.

5 They hunted the hollows all over
   Till at length old Boxer give tongue;
   There's Dido and Ruler and Bonny Lass and Julius,
   So merrily they run her along.

6 Now to speak in praise of those beagles,
   They was as good dogs as ever run in fields;
   For as sure as they move her they are sure to stick her,
   Till they make the poor puss ill.

7 Now ain't this a dainty fine puss?
   She has held us from eleven to one.
   Over hills and high mountains are beagles kept hunting
   Until they pull poor puss down.

SUSSEX

96   The Lawyer

The lawyer of the title is the villain of the piece, and he is trounced by a canny country girl. The brisk realism and salty language have a strong flavour of the eighteenth century, though I have not seen a copy of the song from that early. Vaughan Williams's sprightly version came from a Mr Ted Baines, who was born in about 1834.

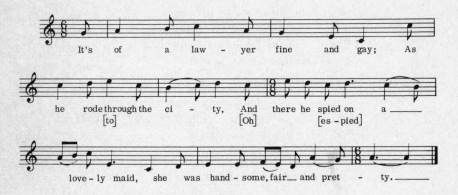

It's of a law - yer fine and gay; As
he rode through the ci - ty, And there he spied on a _____
[to]   [Oh]   [es - pied]
love - ly maid, she was hand - some, fair__ and pret - ty. ____

2 'Good morning unto you, fair maid,
    And where are you a-going?'
    'Down in yonder meadows, green meadows,' said she,
    'Where my father is a-mowing'.

3 The lawyer off his horse did jump,
    Intending for to view her.
    She's given a leap right over the stream,
    For fear he would undo her.

4 The lawyer rode like any deer,
    And then did overtake her;
    And then he did whisper all in her ears
    Of what a fine lady he'd make her.

5 'Come hold your apron up, my dear,
    I'll fill it full of treasures;
    If you will grant me your sweet love,
    One minute or two of pleasure.

6 'So now you come to London', he says,
  'It's there a fine lady I'll make you;
  There you shall enjoy a silken gown,
  Diamond rings, gold chains and gold laces'.

7 'It's I'd sooner be a poor man's wife,
  Sit at my wheel a-spinning,
  Than I would be a lawyer's jade –
  They are the worst of women'.

97   All Things Are Quite Silent

The press gang figured in songs long after it was extinct. However, the language here – poetic diction, euphemisms, the pastoral convention – suggests contemporaneity. The song was noted by Vaughan Williams in 1904, which seems to have been the sole occasion on which it was recovered from oral tradition. It is also rare as a street ballad. The only copy I have seen was issued by J. Ferraby, Butchery, Hull, under the title of 'I'll Mourn for my Sailor; Or, The Compulsion'.

All_ things are quite si-lent, each mor-tal_ at rest, When me and my love__ got snug in__ one nest, When a bold set_ of ruf-fians they en-tered our cave, And they forced my dear je-wel to plough the_ salt wave.

2 I begged hard for my sailor as though I begged for life.
  They'd not listen to me, although a fond wife,
  Saying: 'The king he wants sailors, to the sea he must go';
  And they've left me lamenting in sorrow and woe.

[149]

3 Through green fields and meadows we ofttimes did walk,
And sweet conversation of love we have talked;
With the birds in the woodland so sweetly did sing,
And the lovely thrushes' voices made the valleys to ring.

4 Although my love's gone I will not be cast down.
Who knows but my sailor may once more return?
And will make me amends for all trouble and strife,
And my true love and I might live happy for life.

98   The Carter

A waggoner in the north of England was called a carter in the south.
Both were in charge of horses, not only for pulling carts but also for
ploughing. Their day was lengthened by the need to feed and groom the
horses, both before and after work. Carters nevertheless took immense
pride in their work, as this homemade song shows. The singer was not,
however, a carter, but a cowman, aged about 80. He knew some sixty
songs, learned mostly from his father.

I once was a bold fellow and went with a team, And
all my delight was in keeping them clean; In
keeping them clean, boys, to show their bright colour I
gained a good character by being a good fellow. I
gained a good character by being a good fellow.

2   At every evening I goes to my bed
    The thoughts of my horses comes into my head.
    I rises next morning to give them some meat,
    As soon as I can get my shoes on my feet.

3   I never took delight but in prattling with them,
    I always done the best that I could
    To fill up their bellies and lay down to rest.
    I always did think the right way was the best.

4   The first was a bay horse so soft he did feel;
    The next was a grey horse as soft as the silk;
    The next was a black horse as soft as a mole,
    And the other was a brown horse in diamonds did roll.

5   As I goes a-driving all on the highway,
    When light runs my load I feed them with hay,
    And gives them some water when we comes to a pond;
    After they've drinked, boys, go steady along.

6   My feet grows weary walking by their side.
    I said to my mate: 'I'll set up and ride'.
    And as I was riding I made a new song,
    And as I did sing it you must learn it along.

99   Early, Early in the Spring

A sailor and his sweetheart pledge their love on the eve of his departure. He sends letters during his voyage – to Carthagena – to repeat his vows, but finds on returning that she has married a rich, old miser. He rebukes her for inconstancy, saying he prefers the dangers of war to 'false woman's company', but in her defence she claims not to have received the letters. Thus goes an eleven-verse broadside, entitled 'The Disappointed Sailor' (in W. H. Logan, *A Pedlar's Pack of Ballads and Songs*, Edinburgh, 1869, pp.29–30). Admiral Vernon's attacks on Carthagena in the West Indies took place in 1740 and 1741 (and are described, incidentally, in Smollett's novel, *Roderick Random*), but the song was current for the next 150 years, though sometimes in abbreviated form.

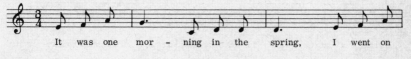

It was one mor - ning in the spring, I went on

board   to   serve the   King.   I ___ left   my   dear - est dear be -

- hind, ___ which   of-ten-times   told   me   her heart was   mine.

2 When I was on the raging seas
   I took all opportunities
   To write letters to my dearest dear,
   But from her I could never hear.

3 I went into her father's hall,
   And loud for my true love I called.
   Her father asked me what I did mean:
   'For she hath long time married been.

4 'She is married for the turn [term?] of life,
   And you must seek some other wife'.
   I'll curse all gold and silver, too,
   And all false lovyers who are not true.

100   Hurricane Wind

Here is another tale of a sailor being jilted for a man of superior wealth. The song has been noted in Vermont and Tennessee, but ours is apparently the only version to have been recorded in England. It is a condensation into one-third the length of 'The Perjured Maid', a Scots chapbook text in 36 verses, and some points are left unclear. The lady's father is 'a nobleman of Exeter'. The letter/note (verse 7/11) is a request by the sailor (a sea captain) not to go ahead with her marriage. When this is ignored the captain drowns himself in the river, then his ghost exercises the right of a dead lover to claim his betrothed: ''Tis not your cries', said he, 'can save/Your perjured body from the grave;/This night you'll lie with me in clay'./Then straight he took her hence away.

'Twas   of   a   migh-ty,   no-ble knight, And he   had   a   daugh-ter, a

[152]

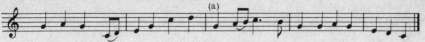

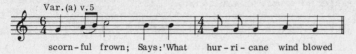

beau-ty bright; And at the age of six-teen years She courted was by lords and peers.

Var.(a) v.5

scorn-ful frown; Says:'What hur-ri-cane wind blowed

2 But none could gain her heart so free
   As a young sea captain who came from sea.
   He was the master of her heart;
   They oft-times vowed they never would part.

3 A piece of gold they broke in two:
   'If ever I do prove false to you,
   May some heavy vengeance fall from above,
   If ever I do slight my love'.

4 This young man went down to the seas,
   Brought home fine tales this maid to please;
   But before six months were scarcely gone,
   Courted she was by another man.

5 As she was a-walking down the street,
   Her young sea captain she chanced to meet.
   She looked at him with a mournful frown;
   Says: 'What hurricane wind blowed you to town?'

6 He looked at her and at last did say [he said]:
   'I hear tomorrow you're going to wed'.
   She looked at him with scorn: 'It's true';
   Says: 'If I am, what's that to you?'

7 She took her letter from his hand,
   And in [with] that letter she gave a laugh;
   She put it into her pocket then,
   And back to her comp'ny returned again.

8 That night was past, the next day drew near;
   To church she went and was married there.
   That day they spent with joy and mirth,
   But mark what sorrows come at last.

9 The day was spent, the night drew near,
   When to her bedroom she did appear,
   And says: 'When you do please to come
   My maid will light you to my room'.

[153]

10 The maid took her leave and she went downstairs,
    And then that young man did appear;
    But he found her chamber all alone,
    And that fair lady she was gone.

11 They searched those rooms and chambers round,
    In her pocket a note they found,
    Which grieves them all the more and more,
    Because 'twas wrote the day before.

12 Now the old man cries and makes his mourn;
    The young man cries: 'I am undone'.
    Now a warning take, both young and old:
    Never break your vows for the sake of gold.

101   The Turtle Dove

Robert Burns wrote of his famous 'Red, Red Rose' that it was originally
'a simple old Scots song which I had picked up in the country' (1794).
The earliest known version was published in England between 1709 and
1714, under the title of 'The Unkind Lovers; or, The Languishing
Lament of the Loyal Lovers'. It survived to the present day as 'The True
Lover's Farewell' or 'The Turtle Dove'. The vow of fidelity is among the
finest passages, not only in traditional song, but in poetry *tout court*.
Unfortunately, its hyperbole of rocks melting and stars falling from the
sky has now, in the nuclear age, taken on an ominous ring. Vaughan
Williams recorded the song on a phonograph from Mr Penfold, the
landlord of the Plough Inn, Rusper. The cylinder has survived, but is
difficult to decipher, and some of the words are conjectural.

'O— fare thee well, my dear-est love, Aye, fare thee well a-

-while. If I roam a-way I'll come back a-gain, If I

roam ten thou-sand miles, my love, If I roam ten thou-sand miles.

2 'Ten thousand miles it is a long way
For to leave me here alone;
To leave me here to lament and sigh,
Where I never shall hear your voice, my dear,
Where I never shall hear your voice'.

3 'Your mourn, my love, I never shall hear,
Nor likewise none of your grief;
On my homeward way I'll come back again
To all my friends that's near, my love,
To all my friends that's near.

4 'The stars will never fall from the sky,
Nor the rocks never melt with the sun;
I never will prove false to the pretty girl I love
Till all those things be done, my dear,
Till all those things be done'.

5 'O yonder do sit that little turtle dove,
He do sit on yonder high tree;
And making a moan for the loss of his love,
As I will do for you, my dear,
As I will do for you'.

102   The Pretty Ploughboy

Although the press gang effectively ceased after 1815, and entirely after
1835, its iron remained in the soul of country singers for a hundred

[155]

years afterwards. The idea of the press gang being used to remove the importunate was by no means fanciful. As Dudley Pope writes: 'In a village or town, "forming the press" was a way of paying off old scores; a rival for a young woman's hand, a jealous mistress, an angry wife – all could rely on the press solving their problems' (*Life in Nelson's Navy*, 1981, pp.123–4). Few pressed men would have a wealthy sweetheart to buy their release.

It's of a pret-ty plough-boy was ga-zing o'er his plough; — His hor-ses stood rest-ing 'neath the shade. —— 'Twas — down in yon-der grove he went whist-ling to his plough. And he chanced there to meet a pret-ty maid.

2 And this was his song as he walked along:
   'Pretty maid, you are of high degree;
   If I should fall in love and your parents they should know,
   The next thing they would send me off to sea'.

3 So when her aged parents they came for to know –
   The ploughboy was ploughing on the plain –
   A press gang they sent and they pressed him away,
   And sent him to the wars to be slain.

4 Then she dressed herself all in her best,
   And her pockets were well lined with gold;
   And she trudged through the streets with tears in her eyes
   In search of her jolly sailor bold.

5 The first that she met was a jolly sailor lad.
   'Have you seen my pretty ploughboy?' she cried.
   'He's just crossed the deep, and sailing for the fleet'.
   Then he said: 'Pretty maid, will you ride?'

6 She rode till she came to the ship her love was in,
   Then unto the captain did complain.
   Said she: 'I'm come to seek for my pretty ploughboy
   That is sent to the wars to be slain'.

7 A hundred bright guineas she freely pulled out,
   And gently she told them all o'er;
   And when she got her pretty ploughboy in her arms,
   She hugged him till she got him safe on shore.

8 And when she got her pretty ploughboy in her arms,
   Where oftentimes he had been before,
   She set the bells to ring, and sweetly she did sing,
   Because she met with the lad she did adore.

told them: counted them

103   The Witty Lass of London

As in 'The Lawyer' (no 96), a poor young woman rejects the venial
sexual advances of a rich man. In so doing, however, she achieves
marriage and attains considerable wealth. The song dates back at least
to the late seventeenth century, when it appeared on a black letter
broadside as 'Beautifull Nancy: or, The Witty Lass of *London*, who by
her withstanding the powerfull Temptations, was lawfully married, and
became an Alderman's Lady. To the Tune of The Gentleman's Frollick'.
In 1778 an American privateersman imprisoned at Forton, near
Portsmouth, copied down a version from some printed source into his
notebook (G. G. Carey, ed., *A Sailor's Songbook*, Amherst, Mass.,
1976, no 45). Another street ballad copy, this time in white letter,
appeared in 1794. The song then vanished from sight until 1904, when
Vaughan Williams noted it from Mrs Harriet Verrall, of Horsham. Her
version is given here, with verses 4 to 6 added from the 1794 sheet. Mrs
Verrall, who died in 1918 at the age of about 63, was a major singer,
with a repertoire of over 50 songs.

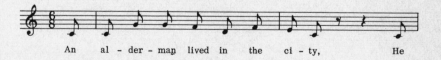

An   al - der - man   lived in   the   ci - ty,   He

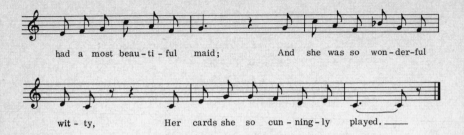

had a most beau-ti-ful maid; And she was so won-der-ful wit-ty, Her cards she so cun-ning-ly played.

2 Her master came to her one morning,
For to tee and to tie on her knee,
Saying how many fine presents he gave her:
'Nancy, my dearest, love me'.

3 'Oh master, I much wonder at you,
A man that's so aged and grey
Should have such a longing desire
A poor innocent maid to betray.

4 'If I should be with child by my master,
And he the same thing should deny,
Then my poor baby must suffer,
While I in prison do lie'.

5 'O Nancy you shall go to your mother,
Who liveth in fair Gloucestershire;
And if the child you should murder
There's no one shall know it, my dear'.

6 'I never will trust you nor try you,
Nor never a man in the place,
So much as one night to lie by me,
And bring me to shame and disgrace'.

7 When he found he could not delude her,
Away to the church they did ride.
Now she's an alderman's lady,
With a footman to ride by her side.

For to tee and to tie on her knee: 'And toyingly tickled her knee' (black letter version)

[158]

A father imprisons his daughter because of her love for a servant man. The song is alternatively known as 'The Cruel Father and Affectionate Lover', 'The Imprisoned Lady', 'The Daughter in a Dungeon' and 'Love Laughs at Locksmiths'. Such a profusion of different titles usually indicates widespread popularity, and the song has been found in Ireland (where it perhaps originated), Canada, and many English counties, though not in the north. Vaughan Williams collected several versions in the south and Midlands, including this one from Mr and Mrs Verrall of Horsham, Sussex. He took down only the tune, so the words have been supplied from a street ballad printed by Harkness in the north of England, at Preston.

It's   of a dam - sel both fair and handsome ; These lines are true,   as I

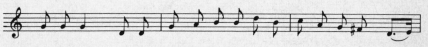

have been told.   Near the   banks of Shan-non in a   lof - ty man-sion   Her—

pa - rents lived,   and had   stores of gold.   Her   hair was black   as a

ra - ven's fea-ther ;   Her   form and fea - tures, des - cribe who can.   But

still it's fol - ly   be - longs to na - ture : She— fell in love with a   ser-vant man.

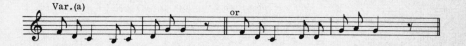

[159]

2 Sweet Mary Ann with her love was walking;
   Her father heard them, and nearer drew;
   And as those true lovers were fondly talking,
   In anger home her father drew.
   To build a dungeon was his intention,
   To part true love he contrived a plan;
   He swore an oath that's too vile to mention
   He'd part that fair one from her servant man.

3 He built a dungeon with brick and mortar
   With a flight of steps, for 'twas underground;
   The food he gave her was bread and water,
   The only cheer that for her was found.
   Three times a day he did cruelly beat her;
   Unto her father she thus began:
   'If I've transgressed now, my own dear father,
   I'll live and die for my servant man'.

4 Young Edwin found out her habitation,
   'Twas well secured by an iron door;
   He vowed in spite of all this nation
   To gain her freedom, or rest no more.
   'Twas at his leisure, he toiled with pleasure
   To gain releasement for poor Mary Ann.
   He gained his object and found his treasure;
   She cried: 'My faithful servant man'.

5 A suit of clothing he bought his lover,
   'Twas man's apparel, her to disguise;
   Saying: 'For your sake I'll face your father.
   To see me here it will him surprise'.
   When her cruel father brought bread and water,
   To call his daughter he then began.
   Said Edwin: 'Enter. I've cleared your daughter,
   And I will suffer, your servant man'.

6 Her father found 'twas his daughter vanished,
   Then like a lion he did roar.
   He said: 'From Ireland you shall be banished,
   Or with my broadsword I'll spill your gore'.
   'Agreed,' said Edwin, 'so at your leisure,
   Since her I've freed, now do all you can.
   Forgive your daughter. I'll die with pleasure.
   The one in fault is your servant man'.

7 When he found him so tender-hearted,
Then down he fell on the dungeon floor.
He said: 'True lovers should not be parted,
Since love can enter an iron door'.
Then soon they joined, to be parted never;
To roll in riches, this young couple can.
This fair young lady, amidst rural pleasures,
Lives blest for ever with her servant man.

105   Cloddy Banks

A young man encountered after a long absence is not recognised by his
true love. He questions her to test her constancy, then reveals his
identity. The theme occurs over and over again in folk songs, and it must
have been a favourite both of singers and their audiences. 'Cloddy' is
Claudy, in Ireland. The song was popular in England, and it also
travelled to Australia.

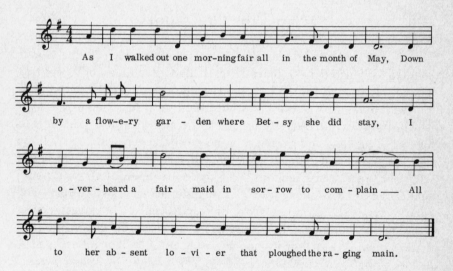

As I walked out one mor-ning fair all in the month of May, Down
by a flow-e-ry gar - den where Bet - sy she did stay, I
o - ver - heard a fair maid in sor - row to com - plain ___ All
to her ab - sent lo - vi - er that ploughed the ra - ging main.

2 I steppèd up to this pretty maid. I said: 'My joy and heart's delight,
How far do you mean to travel, this dark and stormy night?'
'I am in search of a faithful young man, and Johnny is his name.
All on the banks of Cloddy I've been told he does remain.

3 'If my Johnny was here this night he'd keep me free from harm.
He's a-fighting in the battle, all in his uniform.

He's a-fighting the battle his foes to destroy,
Like a rolling prince of honour for this the war of strife'.

4 'It's just six weeks and better since your Johnny left the shore;
He was cruising the wide ocean where the foaming billows roar.
He was cruising the wide ocean for honour and for gain;
I've been told the ship was wrecked and lost all on the coast of Spain'.

5 Soon as she heard the dreadful news she fell into despair,
Wringing her hands and tearing of her hair.
'Since Johnny's gone and left me no man on earth I'll take;
Down to some lonesome valley I'll wander for his sake'.

6 Young Johnny standing hearing of the words he could no longer stand.
He fell into her arms, saying: 'Betsy, I'm the man.
I am that faithful young man who you thought a-once was slain,
And since we've met on the Cloddy Banks we'll never part again'.

for this the war of strife: 'on the banks of Troy' in another version

106   Cupid the Ploughboy

Love once more crosses class barriers, in a song which Baring Gould believed originated in a black-letter ballad of about 1670, entitled 'Cupid's Triumph'. In it, a lady defies Cupid, who causes her to fall in love with and marry a poor man. The moral is: 'If Muck do match with Muck, both will be dirty;/When wit & wealth do truck, nothing can hurt ye:/True-love and Vertue shall do more than crowing will,/I hope Fair Virgins all will take my Counsel'. All very well, but the connection with our song seems tenuous, and there are none of those striking similarities of phraseology which stamp different versions of a particular song through the centuries. Talk of Cupids and of marriages across social divides undoubtedly existed in the seventeenth century, but the earliest record so far, for my money, of 'Cupid the Ploughboy' is in *A Sailor's Songbag*, compiled in 1778–9. The splendid picture of a bare-breasted lady on a heading of 'Cupid's Triumph' is shown on p. xxiii.

As   I   walked out one   May mor-ning when the   May was all in

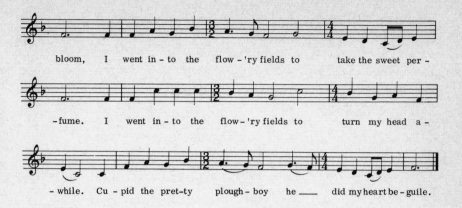

bloom, I went in-to the flow-'ry fields to take the sweet per-
-fume. I went in-to the flow-'ry fields to turn my head a-
-while. Cu-pid the pret-ty plough-boy he ___ did my heart be-guile.

2 As this young man was a-ploughing his furrows deep and low,
   Breaking the clods to pieces, some barley for to sow,
   I wish the pretty ploughboy my eyes had never seen;
   Oh it's Cupid the pretty ploughboy, with his arrows sharp and keen.

3 If I should write a letter, addressed to this young man,
   Perhaps he'd take it scornfully, and say it was in vain.
   Perhaps he'd take it kindly, and write to me again;
   Oh it's Cupid the pretty ploughboy with his arrows sharp and keen.

4 A worthy, rich young gentleman a-courting to me came,
   And because I would not marry him my parents did me blame.
   Adieu, young man, for ever; farewell, farewell, adieu;
   It's Cupid the pretty ploughboy which has caused my heart to rue.

5 Now the ploughboy, hearing this lady most sadly to complain,
   Cried out: 'My dearest jewel, I will ease you of your pain.
   If you will wed with a ploughboy I will for ever prove true:
   It's you my heart have wounded, and I love no one but you'.

6 The lady soon consented to be his lawful bride,
   Then straight unto the church they went, and there the knot was tied;
   And now they live in splendour, for they have gold in store.
   The lady and the ploughboy each other do adore.

107   The Lark in the Morning

A good time at the wake — and also on the way home, featuring a
ploughboy and his sweetheart: this would seem likely to have been the
ideal subject for a ballad. Ballads were sold at wakes, and ploughboys

frequently appeared in them as heroes, and were avid purchasers – the two things not being unconnected. This song was widely printed on ballad sheets, though invariably beginning with a verse which is equally invariably omitted from the many oral versions: 'As I was a-walking one morning in May,/I heard a pretty damsel these words for to say:/"Of all callings whatever they may be,/No life like a ploughboy all in the month of May".'

The lark in the mor-ning she rose from the west, And mounts in the air__ with the dew u-pon her breast; And with the pret-ty plough-boys she'll whis-tle and she'll sing, And the plough-boy is as hap-py as a prince or a king.

2 When his day's work is done that he has for to do,
 Perhaps to some country wake he will go.
 There with his sweetheart he will dance and sing,
 And at midnight return with his lass back again.

3 And as they return from the wake in the town,
 The meadows being mowed and the grass all cut down;
 If chance for to tumble all on the new mown hay,
 It's: 'Kiss me now or never', the damsel will say.

4 When twenty long weeks were over and past,
 Her mammy asked the reason she thickened in the waist.
 'It was the pretty ploughboy', the damsel did say,
 'That caused me to tumble all on the new mown hay'.

5 Come all you pretty maidens wherever you be,
 You may trust a ploughboy to any degree;
 They're used so much to ploughing their seed to sow,
 That under your apron it's sure to grow.

[164]

6 So good luck to all ploughboys wherever they be,
  That will take a pretty lass to sit upon their knee,
  And with a jug of beer will whistle and sing,
  And a ploughboy is as happy as any prince or king.

108   The Banks of the Nile

The song with this title originally referred to Nelson's voyage to Egypt, which led to the Battle of Aboukir Bay, off the mouth of the Nile, in 1798. (It may derive from an earlier song from the time of the American War of Independence.) When a military expedition to Egypt took place, leading to the Battle of the Nile, in 1801, the song was adapted to fit the army rather than the navy. It turned into a powerful plea against war, and became known in Britain and also America, where a Civil War adaptation spoke of fighting 'those Southern soldiers way down upon Dixie's Isle'.

'Hark, I hear the drums a-beat-ing, and, love, I must a-way. I hear the bu-gles call [-ing] me, come, love, I must a-way. We're or-de-rèd from Ports-mouth, it is for ma-ny a mile, To fight the blacks and hea-thens on the banks of the Nile.'

2 'O William, dearest William, don't leave me here to moan [mourn?];
  You'll make me curse and rue the day as ever I was born.
  I will cut off my curly locks and come along with you,
  And dress myself in velveteen; I'll go and see Egypt, too'.

3 'Nancy, lovely Nancy, with me you cannot go.
  Our colonel has given orders no woman for to go.

[165]

We must forget our own sweethearts all on our native isle,
And fight the blacks and heathens on the banks of the Nile'.

4 'Cursed be the wars, my love, and how they first begun,
For they have robbed old Ireland of many a clever one.
They've taken from us our own sweethearts all from our native isle,
And their bodies lie a-mouldering on the banks of the Nile'.

5 'When the wars are over, it's home we will return,
And to our wives and sweethearts we left behind at home.
We'll roll them in our arms until the end of time,
And we'll go no more to battle on the banks of the Nile'.

109   The Gallant *Rainbow*

In many songs, women are condemned to an unfulfilled yearning to go
to sea. Here, a 'young damsel', in some versions identified as Nancy, the
captain's daughter, is not only aboard ship, but takes command when
her father falls in battle. John Masefield assumed in his *Sailor's Garland*
(1906) that the song derived from an encounter with Ward, the pirate
(for whom, see no 54); but there is no evidence, and the protagonists are
never identified in anything more than the vaguest of terms.

As I was a walk - ing down by the Spa-nish shore, The
[sail - ing]
drums_ they did beat _ and the can - non did roar. I
spied a lof - ty ad - mi - ral come bear-ing down the main, Which
caused us to hoist up our top - sails a - gain.
Var.(a)

2 'Now, my lads, be steady; now, my boys, be true.
   To chase this young admiral we quickly will pursue.
   We soon will overtake him all on the ocean wave;
   Without a good protection will give him a broadside'.

3 For broadside, for broadside, it was our full intent;
   We gave them a broadside as good as we could send.
   The very second broadside our captain got slain.
   Up rose a young damsel in his place to remain.

4 We fought for four hours, four hours and more [so severe],
   Till we hadn't scarce a man our own ship could steer;
   Till we hadn't scarce a man that could fire off a gun,
   And the blood from our ship like water did pour [run].

5 'For quarter, for quarter', this admiral cried.
   'No quarter, no quarter', this young damsel replied.
   'These are the best of quarters to you I can afford:
   You must fight, sink, or swim, or jump overboard'.

6 So now the trouble's over we'll drink a glass of wine,
   And you must drink to your true love and I must drink to mine.
   Good health to that young damsel that fought all on the main,
   And here's to the gallant ship, the *Rainbow* was her name.

110   The Rambling Sailor

This light-hearted song of sexual good fortune was once very popular
with country singers. Baring Gould believed it to be a re-make of 'The
Rambling Soldier', but I am inclined to think that the reverse is true.
Whichever the case, both were widely issued on broadsides, but the
'sailor' was by far the more common in oral tradition, with sets of words
moving farther and farther away from the fairly standard printed
version. Vaughan Williams's cylinder recording of Mr Peter Verrall's
singing is still extant, though limited to the first two verses.

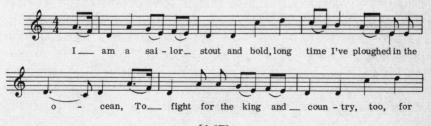

I＿ am a sai-lor＿ stout and bold, long time I've ploughed in the

o - cean, To＿ fight for the king and ＿ coun - try, too, for

[167]

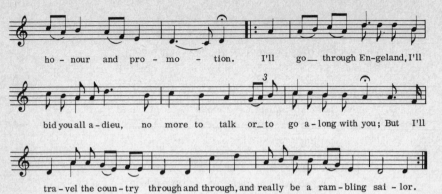

ho - nour and pro - mo - tion. I'll go__ through En-geland, I'll
bid you all a - dieu, no more to talk or__ to go a - long with you; But I'll
tra - vel the coun - try through and through, and really be a ram - bling sai - lor.

2 O when first I came to Reading town, oh there was lasses plenty.
   I boldly steppèd up to one of them to court her for her beauty.
   I said: 'My dear, what do you choose? There's ale and wine and brandy, too,
   And besides a pair of new stuffed shoes, for to travel with a rambling sailor'.

3 When first to Gloucester town I came, the comely lasses were many.
   If I should meet with a pretty gal I'll court her for her beauty.
   I'll whisper softly in her ear: 'My dearest dear, be of good cheer';
   And straight to bed she will prepare, to sleep with a rambling sailor.

4 In the morning when I first arise I'll court her for an hour;
   I'll leave her there to take some rest, or I'll go and court some other.
   If she waits there till I do return, she'll wait there till the day of doom.
   I'll court them all and marry none, for still I'm a rambling sailor.

5 If she should ask to know my name you'll tell her it is young Johnson.
   I have a licence from the queen to court all girls that's handsome.
   With my fond heart and wheedling tongue I'll court them all both old and
        young;
   I'll court them all and marry none, for still I'm a rambling sailor.

111　　　　Duke William

Duke William (who reigned from 1830 to 1837 as King William IV) sets
out to discover how the navy treats its sailors. He should have known
perfectly well, for he served in the navy from 1779 to 1790, rising from
midshipman to rear-admiral. Nelson wrote of him as a strict discipli-
narian, but he was nevertheless popular, partly because of his career as a
sailor, partly because of his support for the Reform Act of 1832. The
song was first printed during William's time in the navy, and frequently

[168]

reissued later. Vaughan Williams's rare oral version came from the prolific singer, Henry Burstow (1826–1916) of Horsham. Vaughan Williams took down from him 33 songs, out of his total repertoire of 420.

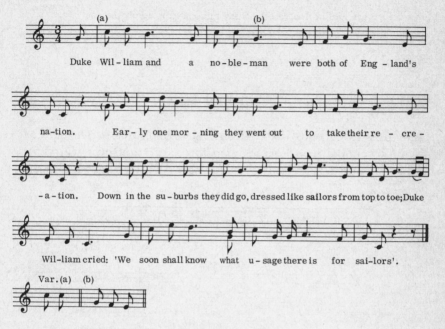

Duke Wil-liam and a no-ble-man were both of Eng-land's na-tion. Ear-ly one mor-ning they went out to take their re-cre-a-tion. Down in the su-burbs they did go, dressed like sailors from top to toe; Duke Wil-liam cried: 'We soon shall know what u-sage there is for sai-lors'.

2 All in a jolly sailor's trim into an inn they entered,
   And soon they did begin to call for white wine and [for] red, sir.
   Before the wine was half drunked out a press gang that was bold and stout
   In the lower room did search about for want of jolly sailors.

3 The landlady said: 'You must go upstairs if sailors you are wanting.
   There is one so fat I dare to say you scarcely can ship him'.
   'Come along, come along', the lieutenant did say,
   'Come along, come along without delay; our warrant runs for sailors.

4 'We do belong to George, our king, pray where is your protection?'
   'I have none at all', the duke replies, 'cast on us no reflection'.
   'Your bold airs and sauciness will surely get your flogging';
   And straightway they did make way for to undress him.

5 'Strip', they cried. The duke replied: 'I do not like your law, sir.
   I never was stripped for to be whipped, so strip me if you dare, sir'.
   But soon they spied a star on his left breast, sir;
   Down on their bending knees did fall, and loud for mercy begged all.
   Duke William cried: 'Base villains all, for using so poor sailors.

[169]

6 'No wonder my father can't get men for to protect his shipping,
   You using them so barbarously, you are always them a-whipping;
   But for the future, great and small, good usage sailors shall have all'.
   May heaven bless that happy day when on was born Duke William.

protection: document protecting holder against impressment
Repeat last line of tune for extra line in verse 5.

112   Creeping Jane

Winning at long odds is the punter's perennial dream. The song is, I think, a fictional frolic, rather than the celebration of a real victory. Henry Burstow's is the only version I have seen which gives a locality.

2 It's when that we came to fair Nottingham
   The people all did say:
   'Poor Jane is not able to gallop over the plain
   And to win the bets that are laid'.

3 When we came to the starting post
   The jockey looked round and he said:

[170]

'If you have a mind to keep my company
I would have you to whip away'.

4 When we came to the first mile post
Poor Jane was still behind;
Then she lifted up her lily-white foot
And tripped it along like a dart.

5 When we came to the second mile post
Poor Jane was still behind;
When the jockey throwed his gropples into her,
But she never did him mind.

6 When we came to the third mile post
Poor Jane was still behind;
But she laid back her ears on her bonny, bonny neck,
And did them all pass by.

7 Now the bets we have won and the money we have got,
And the people all did say:
'Poor Jane she is able to gallop on the plain,
And win the bets that are laid'.

gropples: grapples, spurs

113   Through Moorfields

The hospital of St Mary of Bethlehem was founded in London as early as 1247. Its various sites included, between 1675 and 1814, Moorfields. By the sixteenth century it had provided a new word for the language, 'bedlam', and by the seventeenth was one of the sights of the capital. 'All the afternoon I at the office', wrote Samuel Pepys in 1669, 'while the young people went to see Bedlam'; and Thomas Hutton, who had walked down to London from Derby in 1749 made it his one paying call: 'I wished to see a number of curiosities, but my shallow pocket forbade. One penny, to see Bedlam, was all I could spare.' Mad songs were popular in England from at least as early as *King Lear* (1605–6). Ours dates from the eighteenth century. It is another tale of love thwarted for fear of a misalliance, but triumphing in the end. An apprentice is banished to sea for falling in love with his master's daughter, who in turn becomes distracted, and is confined to Bedlam. The young man returns with money, frees her and marries her.

[171]

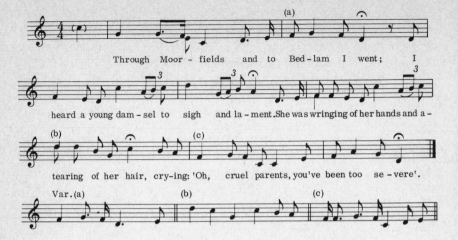

Through Moor - fields and to Bed - lam I went; I heard a young dam - sel to sigh and la - ment. She was wringing of her hands and a - tearing of her hair, cry - ing: 'Oh, cruel parents, you've been too se - vere'.

Var. (a)　　　　　(b)　　　　　(c)

2　'You have banished my true love away to the seas,
　　Which causes me in Bedlam to sigh and to say
　　That your cruel base actions cause me to complain,
　　For the loss of my dear has distracted my brain'.

3　When the silk mercer first came on shore,
　　As he was passing by Bedlam door
　　He heard his true love lamenting full sore,
　　Saying: 'Oh, I shall never see him any more'.

4　The mercer hearing that, he was struck with surprise.
　　When he saw through the window her beautiful eyes
　　He ran to the porter the truth for to tell,
　　Saying: 'Show me the way to the joy of my soul'.

5　The porter on the mercer began for to stare,
　　To see how he was for the love of his dear.
　　He gave to the porter a broad piece of gold,
　　Saying: 'Show me the way to the joy of my soul'.

6　And when that his darling jewel he did see
　　He took her and sat her all on his knee.
　　Says she: 'Are you the young man my father sent to sea,
　　My own dearest jewel, for loving of me?'

7　'Oh. yes, I am the man that your father sent to sea,
　　Your own dearest jewel, for loving of thee'.

[172]

'Then adieu to my sorrows for they now are all fled.
Adieu to these chains and likewise a straw bed'.

8 They sent for their parents who came then with speed;
They went to the church and were married indeed.
Now come all you wealthy parents, and due warning take,
And never strive true lovers their promises to break.

114   The Convict's Lamentation

Moreton Bay was a penal settlement on the Brisbane River in the north
of Australia, founded in 1825. Almost a thousand prisoners were held
there at its peak in 1830, under the command of Captain Patrick Logan,
who was murdered in the same year while out on a mapping expedition.
The song is still well known in Australia, but it has seldom if ever turned
up in oral tradition in Britain. Henry Burstow had a full version, though
the first four lines of verse 6 have been added from elsewhere. The four-
line tune repeated for the eight-line stanzas is a feature of other versions.
Its title is 'Youghal Harbour'.

I__ was born in the land called Eng-land, Late-ly transported from my
na-tive shore; And like Co-lum-bus in his cir-cle sai - ling, I
left be-hind the girl that I a -dore. Through __ Bounding bil-lows that were
loud-ly ra-ging, Like a bold ma-ri-ner my course did steer; Bound
to Ber-mu - da my des-ti-na - tion, Till at length that harbour did soon appear.
Var.(a)

2 There we joined hands in congratulation,
   The safe arrival from the briny waves.
   I soon found out I was mistaken,
   For I was transported to Moreton Bay.
   There every morning as the day was dawning
   To trace from heaven that falling dew,
   Up we all started at a moment's warning
   Our daily labour to renew.

3 As I walked out one summer's morning,
   By the Brisbane water I took my way.
   In silent solitude and meditation
   As I stood watching of the flowing tide,
   I espied a convict loudly complaining,
   While tears of anguish down his cheeks did glide.

4 Saying: 'I have been a prisoner at Port Macquarie,
   In Norfolk Island and Emu Plains,
   In Castle Hill, likewise Toongabbie,
   In all these places I have worked in chains;
   But in all these places of condemnation,
   Each penal station in New South Wales,
   To Moreton Bay I can find no equal:
   Excessive tyranny each day prevails.

5 Now I am bereft of all consolation,
   Yet hopes of liberty for me remain.
   I am behoved in misery and tribulation,
   All there infused by wearing chains;
   Yet I have once more to cross the ocean,
   And leave this station called Moreton Bay,
   Where many a man through downright starvation
   Now lays mouldering in his clay.

6 Like the Egyptians and ancient Hebrews
   We were oppressed under Logan's yoke,
   Till a native black lying there in ambush
   Did give our tyrant his mortal stroke.
   Now fellow prisoners be exhilarated,
   Your former suffering don't bear in mind.
   Where from bondage you are extracted
   You will leave those tyrants far behind.

B.'s wife receives the advances of A., who then finds B. hidden in the cupboard after an encounter with A.'s wife. In other words, A. and B. went to bed with each other's wife. If the plot seems a trifle confused, so is the song, which is nevertheless home-made, very jolly, and apparently unique. The opening of the tune is astonishingly similar to the French revolutionary song, 'Ça ira'.

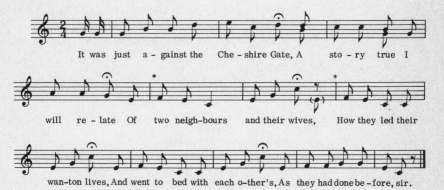

It was just a-gainst the Che-shire Gate, A sto-ry true I will re-late Of two neigh-bours and their wives, How they led their wan-ton lives, And went to bed with each o-ther's, As they had done be-fore, sir.

* Bars between asterisks repeated as necessary to accomodate differing lengths of verses.

2 One of them a journey goes
   But somehow it turned out so
   That he came home before they knew,
   And caught them at their pastime.

3 'Go and fetch me neighbour Brown.
   I don't care if I spend a crown.
   We have some of the best ale in town
   To drive away all sorrow.

4 'If neighbour Brown should not be at home,
   Pray tell his wife she is to come;
   And we will have a bit of fun
   To drive away all sorrow'.

5 He sent his own wife after the ale,
   While they began to frank and frail;
   While they began to frank and frail,
   As they had done before, sir.

6 'Twas up against that cupboard door,
   There he kissed her over and o'er.

There was one in the cupboard it grieved;
It vexed him out of measure.

7　He saw his own wife coming across:
'My dear, I thought you had been lost.
My dear I thought you had been lost,
Or have been to brew it.

8　'It's pour out, wife, and let us drink'.
For poor Brown's wife do little think
There is one in the cupboard who sit and think;
There is one in the cupboard who sit and think,
And know what we have (they've) been doing.

9　'Wife to the cupboard I must go'.
'Husband, dear, do not say so.
They key has been lost some weeks ago;
Pray, therefore do not venture'.

10　But by some means he opened it,
And there he saw his neighbour sit:
'Come out, come out if you think fit.
Pray thee, neighbour, venture'.

11　'Pardon, pardon I do crave'.
'And pardon, pardon you shall have'.
'You have been playing with me the knave.
I've done as much for you, sir'.

12　'Neighbour Brown, put on your hat.
I've only played you tit for tat.
There is no more to be said about that:
I will both lend and borrow'.

frank and frail: there appears to be no meaning in the dictionary for this phrase,
　　though 'frail' as a noun means courtesan, and the meaning of the whole is
　　clear
his own wife coming across: literally; not with the current slang meaning

[176]

WILTSHIRE

116   An Acre of Land

Like 'The Cambric Shirt' (no 17) this derives from a ballad, 'The Elfin Knight' (Child no 2). It seems to have emerged in about the middle of the nineteenth century, and was first printed in *Notes and Queries* (1st ser., VII, 1853, p.8). By this time, wrote Bertrand Bronson, 'the riddles have lost their dramatic function: the story-line is a straightforward recounting, as narrative, of delightful impossibilities, unchallenged by an opponent'.

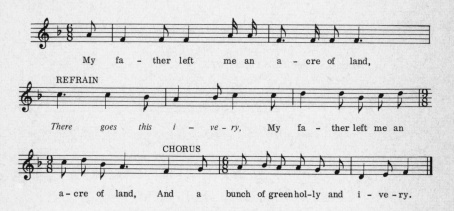

2 I ploughed it with my ram's horn;
   I sowed it with my thimble.

3 I harrowed it with my bramble bush;
   I reaped it with my penknife.

4 I sent it home in a walnut shell;
   I threshed it with my needle and thread.

5 I winnowed it with my handkerchief;
   I sent it to mill with a team of great rats.

6 The carter brought a curly whip;
   The whip did pop and the waggon did stop.

The earliest version of this song which I have seen is on an eighteenth-century ballad slip entitled 'The Maiden's Complaint for the Loss of her Shepherd'. The gentleman in question has the somewhat unlikely name (for a real shepherd, that is) of Strephon; arcadia *à la* Marie Antoinette bulks large; and there is a florid apostrophe to Neptune (to keep the man safe at sea). Nevertheless, there is genuine lyrical feeling: 'To the wake no more you'll take me,/Where the lads and lasses go;/In the garden I ne'er shall meet you,/Where the pretty flowers grow'. Certainly, the song had enough appeal to last for a couple of centuries. One of the best known versions is known as 'The Holmfirth Anthem', because of an arrangement made at the turn of the last century by Joe ('Mendelssohn') Perkins, woolsorter, and conductor of the Holmfirth Choral Society.

2 I boldly steppèd up unto her,
  And she blushed as I drew near;
  I says: 'Fair maid, what is your trouble,
  Or what makes you so lamenting here?'

3 She says: 'Young man, if you will believe me,
My trouble is more than I can bear;
For my true love is gone, is gone and left me,
Across the seas I know not where.

4 'Who is my shepherd I love so dearly,
How can I love him any more?
For he's gone, he's gone, he's gone and he's left me.
I shall never see him again, I fear'.

5 'Twas down in yonder flowery garden,
Where the river runs so bright and clear,
That her cheeks was like two blooming roses
Upon the tree that bud and bear.

YORKSHIRE

118   Young William

Sally, wishing to be discreet, arranges to meet William in the dark. William's captain overhears, substitutes himself for him, and obtains Sally's favours, without either of the lovers being the wiser. A singularly dirty trick, one might think, but everything depends on tone and treatment; and here the approach is jocular. The theme is at least as old as Boccaccio, though this song seems to have been printed first in the early nineteenth century. One copy prescribes the tune, 'Irish Molly'. Vaughan Williams's version was sung by Mr Willy Knaggs at the *Duncombe Arms*, Westerdale, in 1904. There was some difficulty because of his broad Yorkshire accent, and Vaughan Williams was uncertain as to whether the tune should have been in common time. Knaggs was the sexton of Westerdale, and also a 'bass fiddle' player.

CHORUS So＿ here's to ev-ery young man who's fond＿ of a
1. Young Wil-liam was a hand-some, a ro-ving sai-lor

lark, And here's to ev-ery young maid who's up to the
boy, And Sal-ly was the girl he loved, his heart's de-light and

mark;＿ And when her lo-ver press her she will make＿ this re-
joy. He threw his arms a-round her waist when she made this re-

-mark: 'You may kiss me where you will, my love, but kiss me in the dark'.
-mark: 'You may kiss me where you will, my love, but kiss me in the dark'.

2 'Oh, it's not for being kissed by you that makes me afraid,
   But modesty's a game, you know, that's looked for in a maid;
   And prudence teaches simple girls to keep the world blind,
   So they seem to be seem to be saucy when fain they would be kind'.

3 A captain overhearing these lovers discourse,
He thought that he might kiss the girl and she be none the worse.
He heard young William name the time to meet her in the park;
Says he: 'I will go in his stead and kiss her in the dark'.

4 Now the third night after, just at the close of day,
The captain had found out a plan to keep her love away;
With William's dress upon his back he's gone into the park.
He rolled her on the dewy grass and kissed her in the dark.

5 So in full three months after, to William she was wed,
And in full six months after she safely got her bed.
Her husband he did wonder how it came within the mark,
But little he thought the captain had kissed her in the dark.

6 The captain stood godfather unto this lovely boy,
And threw him down five hundred pound which he does now enjoy;
And Sally smiles unto herself when thinking of the park,
Where the captain rolled her on the grass and kissed her in the dark.

park: field

119   I Married a Wife

Laments about unsatisfactory marriages are legion. This variation on the theme does not appear to have turned up other than from Vaughan Williams's singer, Mr John Norton, of Robin Hood's Bay.

I married a wife of late, to my un-hap-py
fate. I took her [for love] as for-tune did prove, And
not for the near-by es - tate. So I'll tell you the way if you
mean what I say, and I hope it will do you no wrong; For it
[heed]

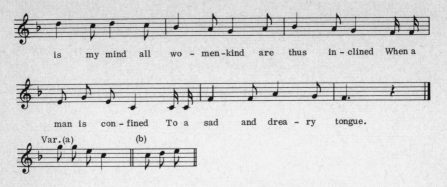

2 Young men, be warned by me, don't pick on a handsome she.
  Take one that is known, and fit for a clown, if neat in her carriage she be;
  For one that will scold she will make you look old, whilst a quiet will make
      you look young.
  For it, *etc.*

120   The Milkmaids

'The Bird in the Bush' is a better-known title for this song, and it sums up and symbolises the action with admirable clarity. One recalls Boccaccio's episode of putting the devil in hell. Vaughan Williams took down the tune and first three verses at Hooton Roberts (a village five miles from Rotherham) from a singer identified merely as 'gypsy'. The rest of the text has been added from a broadside printed at York.

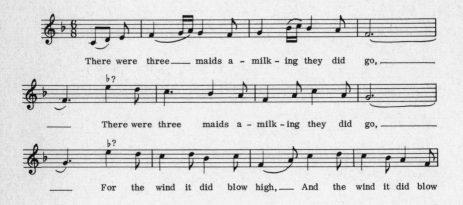

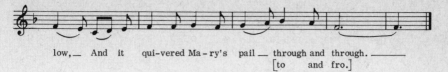

low,— And it qui-vered Ma-ry's pail— through and through. ———
　　　　　　　　　　　　　　　　　　　　[to　　and fro.]

2　O we all met with a man as we knowed,
　　We all met with a man that we knowed.
　　We all did axed him if he had any skill
　　For to catch us a small bird or two.

3　'O yes, we have got a skill,
　　O yes, we have got a skill;
　　And if you will go with me to yonder shady tree
　　I will catch you a small bird or two'.

4　To the merry green wood we all went,
　　To the merry green wood we all went.
　　The birds they did whistle upon every green thistle,
　　For they very well knew their intent.

5　I laid my love under a bush,
　　I laid my love under a tree;
　　He beat at the bush and the bird it flew in:
　　You may very well know what I mean.

6　Here's a health to the bird in the bush,
　　Let it be a blackbird or a thrush.
　　Birds of a feather they will all flock together,
　　Let the people say little or much.

7　Here's health to the jolly dragoon,
　　And send him safely home.
　　We've spent all the day and drunk down the sun;
　　We'll return at the setting of the moon.

121　　　　I Courted an Old Man

On the surface, this is cruel mockery of the old. Yet men have been
known to sing the song with relish, even in their old age, thus showing a
healthy ability to laugh at themselves. Nevertheless, it is very much a
young person's piece.

I courted an old man, It's high down, derry down. I courted an old man, It's high, derry down. I— courted an old man, He swore he would marry me.

Girls, — for your own sake, — never wed an old man.

old man thought his old man thought much of

2 When we were going to church,
  The old man thought his money much.

3 When we first sat down to meat,
  The old man thought much of what we eat.

4 O when we did go to bed,
  The old man lay as he were dead.

5 I laid my hand on his breast,
  The old man swore he'd get no rest.

6 I laid my leg over him,
  The old man swore I'd smother him.

7 When he fell fast alseep,
  Out of bed I did creep.

  New chorus:
  Into the arms of a jolly young man.

8 There we did sport and play,
  Until the break of day.

  Original chorus

thought his money much: his money did begrudge (?)

[184]

SOURCES AND NOTES

List of abbreviations

BL: British Library
Child: F. J. Child, *The English and Scottish Popular Ballads*, 5 vols, 1882–98 (reprinted New York, 1965)
CSH: Cecil Sharp House, London
EBBB: my *Everyman's Book of British Ballads*, Dent, 1980
EBECS: my *Everyman's Book of English Country Songs*, Dent, 1979
JFS: *Journal of the Folk Song Society*, 1899–1931
Laws: G. M. Laws, *American Balladry from British Broadsides*, Philadelphia, 1957
Madden: Madden Collection (of street ballads), Cambridge University Library (microfilm copy at CSH)
Penguin: Ralph Vaughan Williams and A. L. Lloyd, *The Penguin Book of English Folk Songs*, Harmondsworth, 1959
RB: W. Chappell and J. Ebsworth, *Roxburghe Ballads*, 9 vols, Hertford, 1871–1899
Scrapbook: scrapbook of printed and manuscript texts compiled by Vaughan Williams (in Vaughan Williams Memorial Library, CSH)
VW: Vaughan Williams
Wehse: R. Wehse, *Schwanklied und Flugblatt in Grossbritannien*, Frankfurt, 1979

Sources

Material is from BL Add. MSS 54187/91, unless otherwise stated. (A microfilm copy is at CSH, and a complete list of its contents is in M. Kennedy, *The Works of Ralph Vaughan Williams*, 2nd ed, 1966.) I give the precise location of each item (and the place of its first publication), followed by the name of the singer, place and date. Any information on textual emendation then follows, together with references to the classifications of Child, Laws and Wehse. Finally, the number of other items contributed by the same singer is given with published sources listed.

1. The Pride of Kildare
II 182, tune and first verse; Mr Copas (son of the landlady) at *The Chequers*, Cookham Dean, Berkshire; vi 1904. Verses 2 to 6 from broadside no 109,

printed by Stewart, Botchergate, Carlisle (Madden 18/180). Laws P6, 'Pretty Susan, the Pride of Kildare'. VW used the tune in *Six Studies in English Folk Song* (1927).

2. I Had One Man

II 181; Mr Wetherill (tailor), Bourne End, Buckinghamshire; 23 vi 1904. Other versions mentioned in headnote: H. Creighton, *Songs and Ballads from Nova Scotia*, Toronto and Vancouver, 1932, no 90; A. Williams, *Folk Songs of the Upper Thames*, 1923, p.288. Two other songs, including no 3.

3. Bonnie Susie Cleland

II 178, s.n. 'Her father dragged her to a stake' (published in *Journal of the English Folk Dance and Song Society*, 1941, p.79); as no 2. The singer had only one verse (our tenth), with this chorus: 'For she was to be burnt in Nottingham, not far from Nottinghamshire'. The rest of the text has been supplied from Motherwell's *Minstrelsy Ancient and Modern* (1827). Child 65, 'Lady Maisry'.

4. May Song

I 90–1 (with some small variations, in VW, *Eight Traditional English Carols*, 1919, no 5); 'Hoppy' Flack, Fowlmere, Cambridgeshire; 12 vii 1907. Cf 'The Cambridgeshire May-Day Song' (*East Anglian; or, Notes and Queries*, vol IX, 1898, p.245). Three other songs, including 'Lord Ellenwater' (no 5).

5. Lord Ellenwater

I 89; as no 4. Last line in MS reads: 'Shall be given ...'. Child 208, 'Lord Derwentwater'. For a version collected by VW in Hampshire, see JFS III 270–1.

6. The Keeper

III 381; Mr Jim Austin, Little Shelford, Cambridgeshire; 20 viii 1906. In the first verse 'coat', has been substituted for 'arm', 'All' for 'And' (line 3), and 'leaves' for 'lakes'. Original second verse: 'The third doe she run over the lawn/The third doe she made great moan/I tickled her over the merry merry meads'. Text completed from 'The Frolicksome Keeper' (Firth Collection, b 33, Bodleian Library). Cf 'The Huntsman's Delight' (Pepys Collection II 271; RB VII 557–8). Two other songs.

7. The Lousy Tailor

III 389, tune (*English County Songs*, 1908–12, p.92); Mr Gothard, Wilburton, Cambridgeshire; 25 viii 1906. Text: 'The Butcher and the Tailor's Wife', broadside no 501, printed by Harkness, Preston (Madden 18/279), substituting 'lousy' for 'wealthy' in the first line, and with some small amendments. Wehse 319, 'The Butcher and the Tailor's Wife'.

8. The Nine Joys of Mary

I 122 (*A Yacre of Land*, 1961, no 6); Mr Wiltshire (of Fowlmere, Cambridge-shire), at the Workhouse, Royston, Hertfordshire; viii 1907. Five other songs, including 'May Song' (*Folk Songs of the Four Seasons*, 1949).

9. Blackwell Merry Night

III 452, tune only, s.n. 'Bleckel Murry Neet'; Mr Carruthers at Carlisle; 9 viii 1906. Text: adapted from Robert Anderson, *Cumberland Ballads*, 1867 ed., pp.56–8. Six other songs, including 'Geordie Gill' (no 10) and 'King Roger' (no

11). I am indebted to Keith Gregson for information about Carruthers and Anderson, and I have drawn on these books and articles by him: *Cumbrian Songs and Ballads*, Clapham, 1980; 'Bridging the gap: a Cumbrian dialect writer's success in the north-east of England' (in *Journal of the Lakeland Dialect Society*, 1981, pp.7–13); 'Lakeland step-dancing and the Cumbrian bard' (in *English Dance and Song*, vol 42, no 3, 1980, pp.6–7) and 'The Cumberland Bard and Cumberland Ballads' (lecture delivered at CSH, 1981).

10. Geordie Gill
III 457, tune only, s.n. 'Geordie Gair (?)'; as no 9. Text: adapted from Anderson, *op.cit.*, pp.65–6.

11. King Roger
III 453, tune only; as no 9. Text: adapted from Anderson, *op.cit.*, pp.79–80.

12. Down in Yon Forest
I 190 (JFS IV 63; with verse 3 added from elsewhere, in *Eight ... Carols*, 1919, no 4); Mr J. Hall, Castleton, Derbyshire; 1908. Three other songs, including 'And All in the Morning' and 'The Birth of the Saviour' (*Eight*, nos 1 and 7 respectively).

13. The Green Bed
8vo B 15; unspecified singer, the Workhouse, Barnard Castle, Co. Durham; 30 viii 1911. The text taken down by VW is slightly disordered. For example, the first line reads: 'A sailor a sailor of old England (?) a sailor has lately come on shore'. I have omitted some apparently superfluous words, and inserted others to fill lacunae, from a broadside, 'Fortunate Sailor, or, The Green Bed', issued by Jackson and Son of Birmingham (Cecil Sharp Broadside Collection, CSH): v.2, l.2; v.4, l.4: words 'go and'; v.4, l.3; v.5, ll.3,4; v.6, l.2: words 'in this world'; v.8, l.4: words 'For when your money's gone'. Laws K 36, 'Johnny the Sailor'. Wehse 69, 'Liverpool Landlady'. Seven other songs, including 'Franklin's Crew' (no 14), 'Brennan on the Moor' (no 15) and 'Black Frost' (in my *Love is Pleasing*, 1974, no 9).

14. Franklin's Crew
8vo B 16; as no 12. The MS has a fragmentary text of the first verse only. This has been completed, and the rest of the words added, from part of broadside no 751, printed by Harkness, 121 Church Street, Preston (Madden 18/343), under the title of 'Lady Franklin's Lament for her Husband'. Laws K 9, 'Lady Franklin's Lament'.

15. Brennan on the Moor
8vo B 13; as no 12. The text is rather chaotic. Several lines, half-lines and the chorus have been added from broadside no 68, printed by H.P. Such, 177 Union Street, Borough, S.E. (Scrapbook), and what was the second verse in the MS has been moved to become verse 5. Laws L7.

16. Bushes and Briars
4to I 2 (JFS II 143–4); Mr Charles Pottipher (aged about 70, labourer – though described elsewhere by VW as shepherd), Ingrave, Essex; 4 xii 1903. VW, having noted only the first verse, completed the text from a broadside, 'Bushes

and Briers' (sic), issued by W. S. Fortey, Seven Dials (Scrapbook). Original in eight-line stanzas. Twelve other songs, including 'The Pretty Ploughboy' (JFS II 146), 'Princess Royal' (JFS II 145) and 'The Tarry Sailor' (JFS IV 343).

17. The Golden Glove

II 95; Mrs Humphrys (whose age is given as 72 in one note and 75 in another), Ingrave, Essex; 25 iv 1904. VW took down the first verse only; remainder of text from Dixon, pp.107–8. There is a broadside issued by Pitts, 6 Great St Andrews Street, Seven Dials (Scrapbook). Laws N 20. Wehse 17. Seven other songs, including 'The Cambric Shirt' (no 18) and 'Tarry Trousers' (JFS II 153).

18. The Cambric Shirt

II 110; as no 17. The text is (presumably) in the singer's hand. Child 2, 'The Elfin Knight'. See I. and P. Opie, *The Oxford Dictionary of Nursery Rhymes*, 1977 ed., no 86.

19. The New Garden Fields

II 73, tune and first five verses (JFS II 148–9, ditto, with some minor alterations, and three further verses added by VW 'from a Such ballad sheet'); Mr Broomfield (woodcutter), at East Horndon, Essex; 22 iv 1904. Mr Broomfield seems to have come from West Horndon. VW met him both at East Horndon and Herongate. He had sixteen other songs, including 'Old Garden Gate' (no 20) and 'Van Diemen's Land' (EBECS, no 52). VW collected several versions of 'The New Garden Fields', including from Mr J. Punt (for whom, see no 22) of Essex (JFS II 73) and Mr Locke (for whom, see no 70) of Norfolk (JFS IV 334).

20. The Old Garden Gate

8vo A 22–3; Mr Broomfield, West Horndon, Essex; 4 xii 1903. A slightly different version of the same song from the same singer appears in JFS II 152.

21. Robin Hood and the Pedlar

III 417, tune, and 510–12, text; Mr Bell (bricklayer), Herongate, Essex; 16 ii 1906. The text is not in VW's hand. VW noted the tune and text of verse 6 only. Child 132, 'The Bold Pedlar and Robin Hood'. For a version collected by VW from Mr Verrall (for whom, see no 103) in Sussex, see Penguin, p.88. For another version collected in the same county by Mike Yates in 1964, see EBECS no 41. Seven other songs.

22. The Fisherman

II 83; Mr James Punt, East Horndon, Essex; 23 iv 1904. The text is not in VW's hand. Laws O 24, 'The Bold Fisherman'. Seventeen other songs, including 'Keepers and Poachers' (no 23), 'The Three Butchers' and 'Bold Turpin' (EBECS nos 44 and 45), 'The Painful Plough' (*Novello School Songs*, 1912), 'Sprig of Thyme' (VW, *Folk Songs of the Four Seasons*, 1949), 'Lost Lady Found', 'New Garden Fields', 'Newport Street', 'The Cobbler' and 'Died for Love' (JFS II 101, 148, 157, 156 and 158 respectively).

23. Keepers and Poachers

II 294, s.n. 'Good people of England'; as no 22; 26 x 1904. The original of verse 4, lines 2 and 3, reads: 'And one of those night keepers right down he did lay/...
... list'. For 'The Loyal Forrister', see RB VII 763–4.

24. The Merry Green Broomfields

II 296–8, s.n. 'Merry Broom Greenfields'; Mr Kemp (aged about 77), Herongate, Essex; 26 x 1904. Two fragmentary verses have been run together to make verse 5. Verse 3 has been added from Child 43F (adapted). Child 43, 'The Broomfield Hill'. Wehse 2. Two other songs: 'Fountains Flowing' (no 24) and 'Lay still' (a version of 'The Lark in the Morning', JFS II 154). Other versions of 'Broomfield Hill' were collected by VW from Mr Verrall (for whom, see no 103) in Sussex (B. H. Bronson, *The Singing Tradition of Child's Popular Ballads*, Princeton, 1976, pp.110–11), and from Mrs Powell (for whom, see no 46) in Herefordshire (JFS IV 114–15).

25. Fountains Flowing

II 302; as no 24. The original text of verse 5, line 2, reads: 'If one may weep for you poor child, for your own mother'. For the version from Mrs Verrall (for whom, see no 103) of Sussex, which VW adapted for 'To be a pilgrim', see JFS II 202.

26. The Jolly Harrin'

II 49 (*A Yacre*, no 5; with some changes in the text); Mr Ted Nevill, Little Burstead, Essex; 16 iv 1904. Cf S. Baring Gould, *Nursery Rhymes*, 1895, no IV, 'The Herring's Head'. Two other songs, including 'Three Weeks before Easter' (EBECS no 89).

27. The Buffalo

II 246–7; Mr Leary, formerly of Hampshire; now in Almshouses, Castle Street, Salisbury, Wiltshire; ix 1904. The text is in VW's hand in the MS, but there is another copy in his scrapbook which was presumably written by the informant. Verse 2 has been added from broadside no 300, printed by H. Such, 177 Union Street, Boro', S.E. (Scrapbook). One other song: 'Elwina of Waterloo' (no 28).

28. Elwina of Waterloo

II 248–9. s.n. 'The Battle of Waterloo'; as no 27. Part of the text is also in the scrapbook, in the informant's hand. The original verses 2 and 3 have been transposed. Cf broadside no 612, printed by H. Such, 177 Union Street, Borough (Scrapbook).

29. Long Lankin; or, Young Lambkin

MS wanting (JFS II iii–2); Mrs Chidell, Bournemouth, Hampshire; 1902 (via Miss Chidell, 1905). Child 93, 'Lamkin'. One other song: 'Lord Thomas and Fair Eleanor' (JFS II 106).

30. The Constant Lovers

MS wanting (JFS III 294–5), s.n. 'A sailor courted a farmer's daughter'; Mr Henry Day (aged 67), Basingstoke, Hampshire; i 1909. The first three lines of the last verse have been added from a broadside, after F. Purslow (ed.), *The Constant Lovers*, 1972, p.19. Laws O 41. One other song: 'The Dear Irish Boy' (JFS III 311).

31. The Banks of Green Willow

MS wanting (JFS III 292); Mr David Clements (aged 80), Basingstoke, Hampshire; i 1909. The first 6½ verses have been amended from the cylinder recording of the singer preserved at CSH (Tape 267). Child 24, 'Bonnie Annie'. Two other songs: 'The Foggy Dew' and 'Lord Randal' (JFS III 295 and 304). In addition, George Gardiner noted 'The Factory Girl' (Purslow, *op.cit.*, p.29).

32. Robin Hood and the Three Squires

MS wanting (JFS III 268–9); Mrs Goodyear (aged 75), Axford, Hampshire; i 1909. Child 140, 'Robin Hood rescuing three squires'. Wehse 422, 'Robin Hood rescuing the widow's three sons'. Cf broadside, 'Bold Robin Hood', printed by J. Russell, Moor Street, Birmingham (BL Ballads 1876 e 2). One other song: 'Lord Ellenwater' (JFS III 270), and several others collected by George Gardiner, including 'Abroad as I was walking' and 'Old Daddy Fox' (F. Purslow (ed.), *The Wanton Seed*, 1968, pp.6 and 89), and 'Lovely Susan, the Milkmaid' (F. Purslow (ed.), *The Foggy Dew*, 1974, p.54).

33. Fare ye well, Lovely Nancy

MS wanting (JFS III 298–9); Mr George Lovett (aged 68), Winchester, Hampshire; i 1909. Laws K 14, 'Farewell, charming Nancy'. Cf 'The Undaunted Seaman' (RB VII 551). Two other songs noted by George Gardiner were 'Old Mother Crawley' and 'Watercresses' (*Wanton Seed*, pp.91 and 116).

34. Jockey and Jenny

MS wanting (JFS III 310); Mr Alfred Porter (aged 74), Basingstoke, Hampshire; i 1909. George Gardiner collected the same song from Mr Porter in 1906, noting that he was 73 (Hammond Papers, H 593, CSH). The singer did not recall the first two lines of verse 4 on that occasion, either. One other song: 'The American Stranger' (JFS III 309). One other collected by Gardiner: 'T stands for Thomas' (*Wanton Seed*, p.109).

35. God Bless the Master

MS wanting (JFS III 261); Mr Daniel Wigg (aged 84), Preston Candover, Hampshire; i 1909. Two other songs: 'Pretty Nancy' (no 36) and 'Nelson's Monument' (no 37). Three further songs collected by Gardiner: 'The Bricklayer's Dream' and 'The Ploughboy's Dream', with which cf no 94 (F. Purslow (ed.), *Marrowbones*, 1965, pp.12 and 69), and 'When this old hat was new' (*Foggy Dew*, p.95).

36. Pretty Nancy

MS wanting (JFS III 272); as no 35. The first verse only is given; the remainder of the text has been supplied from the Hammond Papers (H.744, CSH; collected by George Gardiner from Mr Wigg in vii 1907). Cf 'Pretty Nancy of London' in *Lord Anson's Garland* (Harding Collection, A 3 (5), Bodleian Library).

37. Nelson's Monument

MS wanting (JFS III 273, s.n. 'Nelson'); as no 35. The first verse only is given; the remainder of the text has been supplied from broadside no 153, printed by Harkness of Preston (Madden 18/683). Another text, from William Fiske, is in the scrapbook.

38. The Lowlands of Holland

MS wanting (JFS III 307); Mr William Bone (aged 66 or 67), Medstead,

Hampshire; i 1909. Child 92. Two other songs: 'The Drowned Sailor' (no 39) and 'The Baffled Knight' (JFS III 257). In addition, Gardiner collected 'The Female Drummer', 'Haymaking Courtship', 'The Roving Batchelor' (*Wanton Seed*, pp.41, 51 and 100), and 'Polly Vaughan' (*Marrowbones*, p.70).

39. The Drowned Sailor
MS wanting (JFS III 258–9, s.n. 'In London fair city'); as no 38. Laws K 18, 'Scarborough Sand'. Cf 'Captain Digby's Farewell', Dryden's poem (*The New Academy of Compliments*, 1671), which was expanded into the ballad, 'Love and Honour' (RB VI 36). See also 'The Sorrowful Ladies' Complaint' (RB IV 398) and 'Stow Brow', broadside no 198, printed by W. Forth, 63 Waverley Street, Hull (Wilberforce Collection, Hull Public Library).

40. Riding Down to Portsmouth
8vo D 34, tune only; Mrs Esther Smith, The Homme, Dilwyn, Herefordshire; ix 1912. Mrs Smith's grave is in Weobley Churchyard. Text: broadside printed by William M'Call (1822–90), 4 Cartwright Place, Byrom Street, Liverpool (Collection of Liverpool Street Ballads, p.70, Liverpool Record Office). Wehse 215. Ten other songs, including 'On Christmas Day' (no 41), 'My mother sent me for some water' (*Love is Pleasing*, 1974, no 2, s.n. 'Collier Lads'), 'Christmas now is drawing near', 'There is a fountain of Christ's blood' and 'God rest you, merry gentlemen' (E. M. Leather and RVW, *Twelve Traditional Carols from Herefordshire*, 1920, nos 3, 4 and 6). For songs collected from Mrs Smith's daughter, May Bradley, see F. Hamer, *Garners Gay*, 1967. For a recent recording from a gypsy now settled in Sussex of 'Riding down to Portsmouth', see *Sussex Harvest* (Topic 12T258, 1975).

41. On Christmas Day
8vo D 3, tune only (*Twelve ... Carols*, no 8, tune and text) as no 40.

42. Dives and Lazarus
MS wanting (JFS IV 47, verses 1 and 14–17); Mr John Evans, Dilwyn, Herefordshire; i 1907. Verses 2–13 from broadside printed by Charles Heath, The Square, Monmouth (Pilley Collection, Hereford City Library). Child 56.

43. The Carnal and the Crane
I 282, tune (JFS IV 22, tune and text); Mr Hirons (aged 60), The Haven, Dilwyn, Herefordshire; 27 vii 1909. Child 55. Three other songs: 'The Angel Gabriel', 'Our Saviour's Love' (*Twelve Carols*, nos 5 and 11) and 'The Unquiet Grave' (*Journal of the English Folk Dance and Song Society*, 1941, p.49).

44. The Bitter Withy
8vo D 21; Mr Morris, Almeley, Near Weobley, Herefordshire; ix 1912. One other song: 'The Rocks of Scilly' (no 45). Verse 4, line 2, reads: 'When you come home at night'. For five other versions of 'The Bitter Withy', including one from William Colcombe (for whom, see no 46), see E. M. Leather, *The Folklore of Herefordshire*, 1912, pp.181–4.

45. The Rocks of Scilly
8vo D 22, s.n. 'Come all you jolly seamen'; as no 44. The first line of verse 1 and the first two lines of verse 5 have been added from the broadside printed by J.

Kendrew, Colliergate, York (York Publications, p.89, BL 1870 c 2). Laws K 8.

46. A Brisk Young Sailor
I 284, tune (JFS IV 122, tune and text); Mr William Colcombe (1827–1911), Weobley, Herefordshire; vii 1909. Five other songs: 'The Sinner's Dream', 'The Outlandish Knight', 'God rest you, merry gentlemen' (JFS IV 122, 18 and 24), 'The Bitter Withy' and 'The Moon Shines Bright' (*Folklore of Herefordshire*, pp.181 and 193). In addition, Mrs A. M. Webb collected at least three more songs: 'There is a Fountain', 'Young Lankin' (*ibid.*, pp.197 and 199) and 'Lord Bateman' (L. Jones, *A Nest of Singing Birds*, n.p., 1978, p.56).

47. The Myrtle Tree
I 286, tune; Mrs Ellen Powell, Westhope, Near Weobley, Herefordshire; vii 1909. Text: verses 1 and 3: also from Mrs Powell, in Mrs E. M. Leather's handwriting (Scrapbook); verses 2, 4 and 5: from the broadside, 'Flash Company, printed by Jackson and Son, Moor Street, Birmingham (Crampton Collection, vol. 4, p.2, BL 11621 h 11). Ten other songs, including 'The Blacksmith' (no 48) and 'Merry Green Broomfields' (JFS II 114; see no 23). In addition, a version of 'The Milkmaid's Song' appears in Leather, *op.cit.*, p.205. It was noted by VW from a phonograph recording made in 1907, when Mrs Powell was living at Canon Pyon.

48. The Blacksmith
I 287, tune (JFS IV 280); as no 47. Text: Penguin, p.22. Mrs Powell's verse: Scrapbook, p.57. Cf Such broadside (Cecil Sharp Collection).

49. The Drowsy Sleeper
8vo E 9, s.n. 'O who is that?'; Mr Saxton, at Pool End, Near Ashperton, Herefordshire; 16 ix 1913. Laws M 4. Two other songs.

50. O Who is That?
8vo E 6; Mr Loveridge, Junior, at camp near *The Trumpet*, Ashperton, Herefordshire; 16 ix 1913. Verse 1, line 3 in MS begins: 'over houri-ri and'. Cf 'John's Earnest Request' (RB VI 202). Two other songs, both with Mr Loveridge, Senior.

51. Wassail Song
8vo D 18; Mr Dykes, near Weobley, Herefordshire; ix 1912. Four other songs, including 'One, O' (EBECS no 146).

52. Orange and Blue
III 88; Mr and Mrs Truell, Gravesend, Kent; 31 xii 1904. One other song: 'John Reilly' (JFS II 214; see no 56).

53. The Captain's Apprentice
III 142, verses 1 to 4 and 7 (JFS II 161–2); Mr James Carter (fisherman, aged about 70, died c. 1915), North End, King's Lynn, Norfolk; 9 i 1905. Verses 5 and 6: Scrapbook. Seven more songs, including 'Ward the Pirate' (no 54) and 'The Blacksmith' (EBECS no 6; not a version of no 47 here). I am indebted to Edgar Samuel for his article, 'Vaughan Williams and King's Lynn' (*English Dance and Song*, Vol. 34, no 3, 1972, pp.92–6), and also for communicating his unpublished, 79-page paper with the same title, written in 1971. See also

Elizabeth James, 'James Carter, Fisherman of King's Lynn', in *English Dance and Song*, vol. 39, no 1, 1977, pp.10–11.

54. Ward the Pirate

III 144 (JFS II 163–4); as no 53. Child 287, 'Captain Ward and the *Rainbow*'. This was also sung by Mr John Bayley of King's Lynn, who had won a prize with it at 'a cheap-jack's singing match', and described it as a 'master-song'. Cf 'The Famous Sea-Fight' (RB VI 426).

55. Spurn Point

III 167, tune, s.n. 'Come people all' (JFS II 178, tune and first verse); Mr Leatherday (sailor), The Union, King's Lynn, Norfolk; 9 i 1905. Verses 2–9 added from broadside no 2, 'Industry off Spurn Point', printed by W. Forth, Waverley Street, Hull (Wilberforce Collection, Hull Public Libraries). Two other songs, including 'On Board a Ninety-Eight' (JFS II 176).

56. John Reilly

III 152; Mr Anderson (fishermen, aged about 70), The Union, King's Lynn, Norfolk; 9 i 1905. VW took down only verses 5 and 6. Remainder from broadside printed by H. P. Such, 177 Union Street, Borough, S.E., under the title of 'Riley the Fisherman' (Kidson Collection, Mitchell Library, Glasgow). Laws M 8, 'Riley's Farewell'. Eleven other songs, including 'Young Henry the Poacher' (no 57), 'The Yorkshire Farmer', 'The Basket of Eggs', 'Erin's Lovely Home', 'The Sheffield Apprentice', 'The Bold Robber', 'Died of Love' and 'The Bold *Princess Royal*' (JFS II 174, 103, 167, 169, 165, 168 and 170 respectively). For another version of 'John Reilly' collected by VW from Mr and Mrs Truell (for whom, see no 52) in Kent, see JFS II 214.

57. Young Henry the Poacher

III 156, first verse (JFS II 166); as no 56. Remainder of text from broadside printed by Pitts, Wholesale Toy and Marble Warehouse, 6 Great St Andrew Street, Seven Dials (Madden 9/656). VW noted: 'The complete words, which are of no great interest, are on a Such ballad sheet'.

58. Edward Jorgen

III 208; Mr Harper, King's Lynn, Norfolk; 13 i 1905. Seven other songs, including 'Just as the Tide was flowing' (no 59), 'Oxford City' and 'The Bonny Boy' (JFS II 162 and 82 respectively).

59. Just as the Tide was flowing

III 200 (JFS II 173); as no 58, but 14 i 1905. VW took down the words of verses 4 and 5 only, in the case of each of which I have placed the second couplet first. The first three verses have been added from a broadside copy (after F. Kidson, *Traditional Tunes*, 1891, p.109). For a full oral version, see M. Karpeles, *Cecil Sharp's Collection of English Folk Songs*, 1974, no 385.

60. The *Cumberland's* Crew

III 189–90; Mr Crist, The Union, King's Lynn, Norfolk; 11 i 1905. Eight other songs, including 'The Loss of the *Ramillies*' (no 61), 'John Raeburn' (no 62), 'A Dream of Napoleon' (no 63) and 'Spanish Ladies' (JFS II 179).

61. The Loss of the *Ramillies*

III 172; as for no 60, but 9 i 1905. Laws K 1. For further information on the wreck, see my article, 'A Storm, a Shipwreck and a Song' (in *Folk Review*, September, 1976, pp.12–13) and G. J. Marcus, 'The Loss of the *Ramillies*' (in *Royal United Service Institution Journal*, vol. 105, pp.510–14).

62. John Raeburn

III 183–4 (JFS II 180–1); as no 60, but 10 i 1905.

63. A Dream of Napoleon

III 162; as no 60. Four lines (verse 3, 1 and 2, and verse 4, 3 and 4) have been added from broadside no 141, printed by Harkness of Preston (Madden 18/671).

64. The Tarry Sailor

4to I 41, tune, s.n. 'So late it was', and 41, fragmentary text, presumably in the hand of the singer, s.n. 'Tarry Sailor' (JFS IV 88, tune and part of verse 1, s.n. 'Jack the Sailor'); Sally Brown, Ranworth, Norfolk; 17 iv 1908. Text completed from broadside, 'Tarry Sailor', printed by Kendrew, Colliergate, York (York Publications, p.205). This is not Laws K 37/Wehse 71.

65. Homeward Bound

III 214–15, s.n. 'Our anchor's weighed'; Mrs Betty Howard, King's Lynn; 10 and 11 i 1905. Two other songs: 'The Sheffield Apprentice' and 'Ratcliffe Highway' (JFS II 169 and 172).

66. Lovely on the Water

I 137 (JFS IV 84); Mr Hilton, South Walsham, Norfolk; 11 iv 1908. Verses 5, 6 7 (part), 13 and 14 added from broadside no 231, 'Henry and Nancy, or, The Lover's (sic) Seperation (sic)', printed by Harkness of Preston (Madden 18/212). The original sheet has seven four-line stanzas. Twelve other songs, including 'The Holly Twig' (no 67), 'Jones Ale' (EBECS no 117) and 'The Outlandish Knight' (JFS IV 123).

67. The Holly Twig

I 139, s.n. 'When I was a bachelor' (my *Love is Pleasing*, 1974, no 33, s.n. 'A Week's Work Well Done'); as no 66. The chorus has been expanded, since VW noted only these words: 'fol de lol lol'. (Laws Q 6). Garland: *West Country Garland*, BL 1161 b 11.

68. Bold Carter

III 116; Mr Whitby (aged about 50, sexton), Tilney All Saints; 7 i 1905. Cf *Irish Boy's Garland*, Harding Collection, Chapbooks A 1, Bodleian Library. Nine other songs, including 'Early in the Spring' (*Yacre*), 'The Yorkshire Bite' and 'Maria Marten' (JFS II 118 and 174).

69. Trot Away

8vo C 4–5; Mr Tuffs, Senior, near Diss, Norfolk; 19 xii 1911. Cf broadside, 'The Trotting Horse', printed by W. Ford, York Street, Sheffield (Harding Collection, Quarto Street Ballads, Bodleian Library). Two other songs.

70. Liverpool Play

I 452; Mr Locke, Rollesby, Norfolk; 26 x 1910. VW took down only the tune, since he had a copy of the words, sent by J. B. Cooding of Southwold, Suffolk, in viii 1910. He noted one variation from this set by Mr Locke, which has been incorporated. I have made a few further, minor alterations for the sake of fitting the words to the music. Eleven other songs, including 'The Man of Birmingham Town' (no 71), 'New Gardens Fields' (JFS IV 334), 'Dark-eyed Sailor' and 'Just as the Tide was flowing' (VW, *Five English Folk Songs*, 1913, no 3).

71. The Man of Birmingham Town
I 145 (JFS IV 85–6); as no 70. The song appeared with some amendments, a rearranged verse order, and the addition of two stanzas (verses 8 and 9 here) from another Norfolk singer, Harry Cox (from JFS VII 8–9) in Penguin, pp.68–69, under the title of 'The Man of Burningham Town', and I have largely followed this pattern.

72. Horse Race Song
8vo C 20; Mr Noah ('Blue') Fisher, at the *Horseshoes Inn*, Tibenham, near Diss, Norfolk; 10 xii 1911. The song was simultaneously noted by VW and George Butterworth. The latter's transcription appeared in *Folk Music Journal*, 1976, pp.109–110. Five other songs, including 'Bonny Robin' (no 73).

73. Bonny Robin
8vo C 24; as no 72. Again collected simultaneously by George Butterworth, whose transcription appears in M. Dawney (ed.), *The Ploughboy's Glory*, 1977, p.8, s.n. 'As Robin was driving'. Cf 'Gee Ho Dobbin': V. de Sola Pinto and A. E. Rodway, *The Common Muse*, 1965, no 154, after J. S. Farmer, *Merry Songs and Ballads*, 5 vols, 1897; vol. 2, p.202.

74. The Keys of My Heart
8vo C 11, s.n. 'Keys of Heaven'; unspecified singer [Mr Woods], Tibenham, Norfolk; 19 xii 1911. Again collected simultaneously by Butterworth, who noted the singer's name. His version appears in Dawney, *op.cit.*, pp.26–7. VW's MS omits the last verse, which has been restored from Butterworth.

75. Lullaby
III 371; Mr Thompson, Dunstan, Northumberland; 7 viii 1906. Three other songs, all learned by the singer from his mother: 'Willy Foster' (no 76), Psalm 23 (metrical version) (*Yacre*, no 8), and 'Over the Hills' (*Yacre*, no 9 = 'Molly of the North Country', in J. Holloway and J. Black, *Later English Broadside Ballads*, 1975, no 79). Two further tunes, and one song; with his wife.

76. Willy Foster
III 375 (*Yacre*, no 4); as no 75.

77. Bizzoms
II 212; Mr Brice (carter, aged about 45), 'came from Crewkerne but now living at Stratford Torrey, near Salisbury, Wiltshire'; 31 viii 1904. The first couplet in both verses 4 and 5 has been added from a broadside, 'Buy Broom Besoms', printed by J. Catnach, 2 Monmouth Court, Seven Dials (Madden, after J. Holloway and J. Black, *Later English Broadside Ballads*, vol. 2, 1979, no 15). One other song.

78. Eggleston Hall

I 4; Mr Warner; at the *Shoulder of Mutton*, Hadleigh, Suffolk; 1 ix 1907. There are some gaps in the MS, possibly because VW had difficulty in keeping up with the singer. I have inserted the necessary words. For a Sussex version collected by Bob Copper, see my EBBB, no 70: 'Epsom Races'.

79. Wild and Wicked Youth

I 365, s.n. 'In London Town'; Mr Robert Hurr, Southwold, Suffolk; 24 xi 1910. Laws L 12, 'The Rambling Boy'. Three other songs, including 'The *Royal George*' (no 80), and one concertina tune.

80. The *Royal George*

I 356; as no 79, except that singer's name not in MS. Collected simultaneously by VW and Butterworth, whose MS supplies the name. The text in VW's MS is not in his own hand.

81. Jack Tar

I 12, s.n. 'Come all you roaring boys'; from 'a man from Stepney' in the workhouse at Hadleigh, Suffolk; 3 ix 1907. Last line wanting in MS. Laws K 39.

82. Lovely Joan

(a) I 354, tune (JFS IV 330, tune, v.1, vv. 5–6, 7 (part) and 8 (part); (b) I 370 = 8vo C 25, v.3; Mr William Hurr (aged about 60 in 1910), Southwold, Suffolk; (a) 24 x 1910; (b) 22 xii 1911. Collected jointly with Butterworth, who gives the date x 1910, and includes the tune and v.3 only in his MS (no 108). The text of vv. 2, 4, 5, 6, 7 (first couplet) and 8 (second couplet) has been added from a broadside without imprint (Mike Yates Collection). Verse 6 in the JFS text has been dropped. It reads: 'Then she mounted on her milk-white steed/ And soon overly she rode/She rode she rode all alone/Until she came to lovely Joan'. Child 112, 'The Baffled Knight'. Wehse 43. Five other songs, including 'The Loss of the *London*' and 'The London Apprentice' (JFS IV 331 and 332).

83. The Dew is on the Grass

I 8; Mr Jake Willis (a veteran of the Crimean War and Indian Mutiny), Hadleigh, Suffolk; 3 and 4 ix 1907. V.4, l.1 in MS: last word is 'gate'. V.4 (second couplet) and vv.5–8 added from broadside without imprint, entitled 'New Mown Hay' (Holloway and Black, vol. 2, no 12). Child 112, 'The Baffled Knight'. Wehse 37C. Eight other songs, including 'The Basket of Eggs' (no 84) and 'Broadstriped Trousers' (no 85). For a version collected by VW in Hampshire, see JFS III 257.

84. The Basket of Eggs

I 6; as no 83. Cf garland: Harding Collection, Chapbooks A. 15, no 19, Bodleian Library. Wehse 196. Other published versions collected by VW from Mr Anderson (for whom, see no 56) of Norfolk, and Mr Henry Burstow (for whom, see no 111) of Sussex (JFS II 102–3).

85. Broad-striped Trousers

I 7 (JFS IV 328, tune only); as no 83. VW commented: 'I have noted the following tune to the same words [as a version of 'Tarry Trousers', sung by Mrs

Verrall (for whom, see no 103) and collected by Francis Jekyll (JFS IV 327)], substituting, however, "soldier" for "sailor" and "broad-striped trowsers" for "tarry trowsers".'

86. The Red Running Rue
I 186, tune and verses 1 and 6; Mr Billy Waggs, Orwell, Suffolk; 13 vi 1908. Remainder of text from VW, *Folk Songs of the Four Seasons*, 1949, no 2. Two other songs.

87. The Barley Straw
I 368, s.n. 'It's of a rich old Farmer'; unspecified singer, Southwold, Suffolk; 24 x 1910. Verses 5 to 8 adapted from 'The Jovial Tinker' in *Lango-Lee's Garland*, printed in Darlington (Harding Collection, Chapbooks A. 5, no 10, Bodleian Library). Cf 'The Jovial Tinker and Farmer's Daughter' (BL 1346 m 7, 31). See also 'The Ragged Beggarman' (my *Everyman's Book of British Ballads*, 1981, no 116).

88. The Lads of Kilkenny
II 131; Mrs Berry ('who learnt it from her father'), Leith Hill Farm, Surrey; v 1904. The MS has only lines 1, 2 and 4 of verse 1. Remainder of text from broadside no 3, 'The Boys of Kilkenny', printed by Harkness of Preston (Madden 18/529). For Lucy Broadwood's note, see JFS III 54.

89. The Ranter Parson
II 290, tune and v.1; Mr Earle (labourer, aged 61, who 'learnt most of his songs off "ballets" or from his father'), Leith Hill Place, Surrey; ix or x 1904. Vv. 2–10 from broadside no 68, printed by T. Ford, Irongate, Chesterfield (Derby Public Library). Wehse 73, 'The Ranting Parson; and the Cunning Farmer's Wife'. Three other songs.

90. High Germany
I 230 (my *Rambling Soldier*, 1977, pp.154–5, s.n. 'The True Lovers'); Mr Flint (shepherd, aged 71; originally from West Grinstead, Sussex), at Lyne, Surrey; 7 viii 1908. The last line of v.3 and the last two lines of v.4 have been added from a broadside, 'The True Lovers; or, The King's Command', printed by J. Whiting, Moor Street, Birmingham (BL 1876 e 3). Six other songs, including 'The Sailor Boy' (no 91) and 'Salisbury Plain' (JFS IV 324).

91. The Sailor Boy
I 131, s.n. 'Down by some river'; as no 90, but 20 viii 1907. Laws K 12.

92. Horn Fair
III 68, tune (JFS II 204, tune and vv.1–3 and 5); Frederick Teal, at the *Wheatsheaf*, Kingsfold, Surrey; 23 xii 1904. There are five verses of text in the scrapbook, presumably in the hand of the informant. The one omitted in JFS has been restored here as v.4.

93. The Grenadier and the Lady
4to I 26, s.n. 'The Dragon and the Lady'; Mr Garman (labourer, aged about 60), Forest Green, Ockley, Surrey; xii 1903. The singer's text (marked 'unfinished', which suggests that VW did not have time to copy it out) was: 'Says the dragon to the lady it is time to give o'er/Says the lady to the dragon

play me one tune more/For I like to hear your music, hear the trinkling of the stream/But I like it much better love to hear the nightingale sing'. I have used instead a text from the scrapbook, in VW's hand. Laws P 14, 'The Nightingale'. Five other songs, including 'The Ploughboy's Dream' (no 94), 'Hunting Song' (no 95) and 'The Cruel Father' (JFS II 98).

94. The Ploughboy's Dream
4to I 18 (JFS II 203); as no 93. VW took down vv.1–2 only, noting: 'unfinished'. Vv.4–6 have been added from broadside printed by J. Paul and Co., 2 and 3 Monmouth Court, Seven Dials (St Bride Printing Library). Cf copy printed by W. S. Fortey, Monmouth Court, Bloomsbury (British Museum, c 270 acqu. 1954 3.6.79). For a version collected from Mr Daniel Wigg (for whom, see no 34) by George Gardiner, see *Marrowbones*, p.69.

95. Hunting Song
4to I 22; as no 93.

96. The Lawyer
II 354; Mr Ted Baines (labourer, aged about 70), Plummer's Plain, Lower Beeding, Sussex; 22 xii 1904. Last line of v.7 in MS reads: 'Or to be in a place of warning'. Two other songs, including 'All Things' (no 97).

97. All Things are quite Silent
II 351 (JFS II 202); as no 96. Broadside: printed by Kendrew (York Publications, p.190, BL).

98. The Carter
II 166 (words, less v.3, and with a different tune, published in RVW, *A Selection of Collected Folk Songs*, 1912, p.29); Mr Stacey (cowman, aged about 80), Hollycombe, Sussex; 28 v 1904. Four other songs, including 'Early, Early in the Spring' (no 99), 'Shipcrook and Black Dog' (EBECS no 83) and 'The Tarry Sailor' (JFS IV 343).

99. Early, Early in the Spring
II 170–1; as no 98. Laws M 1.

100. Hurricane Wind
I 242; Mr David Penfold (landlord), *The Plough Inn*, Rusper, Sussex; 13 ix 1908. Verse 1, second couplet, added from broadside entitled 'The Perjured Maid' (Harvard University Library; reprinted in M. E. Henry, *Folk Songs from the Southern Highlands*, New York, 1938, pp.149–52). Laws P 32, 'A Gentleman of Exeter'. Six other songs, including 'The Turtle Dove' (no 101) and 'The Pretty Ploughboy' (no 102).

101. The Turtle Dove
III 435, tune (JFS IV 267, tune and part of text); as no 100, but 2 and 4 v 1907. Text filled out from VW's phonograph recording of singer (Tape 267, CSH).

102. The Pretty Ploughboy
I 246 (JFS IV 308), tune only; as no 100, but 13 viii 1908. Text added from broadside no 488, printed by Harkness of Preston (Madden 18/276). Laws M 24, 'The Jolly Ploughboy'. For a version sung by Mr Charles Pottipher (for whom, see no 15), see *Yacre*, no 13.

103. The Witty Lass of London

II 144, s.n. 'An Alderman lived in the city' (tune and first verse in VW's hand; four verses of text presumably in informant's hand); Mrs Harriet Verrall (aged about 50; died in 1918 at the age of about 63), Monks Gate, Horsham, Sussex; 24 v 1904. Vv.4–6 added from broadside without imprint, but 'Sold at 42 Long Lane', entitled 'The Alderman and his Lady' (Madden 4/36). Cf 'Beautiful Nancy' (Lord Crawford Collection, now in the John Rylands University Library, Manchester). A total of 48 songs was collected by VW from Mrs Verrall and her husband, Peter. Mrs Verrall sang 24 on her own and 21 with her husband, who sang only three alone. They include (Mrs Verrall) 'The London Prentice' (my *British Ballads*, no 119), 'It's of an Old Couple' (EBECS no 102), 'Mÿ Boy Billy' (*Novello School Songs*, 1912), 'A Sailor in the North Country' (JFS II 194), 'Banks of the Nile' (no 108), 'I've lived in Service' (EBECS no 37), 'Covent Garden' (JFS II 195), 'The Lark in the Morning' (no 107), 'On Christmas Night', 'Our Captain Calls', 'Fare thee well', 'Oxford City' (JFS II 127, 202, 201, 200), 'The Outlandish Knight' (JFS IV 121); (both) 'Rolling in the Dew' (JFS IV 284), 'Cupid the Pretty Ploughboy' (no 106), 'The Young Servant Man' (no 104), 'Salisbury Plain' (EBECS no 47), 'Jolly Thresherman' (JFS II 198), 'The Gallant *Rainbow*' (no 109), 'Jolly Ploughboys', 'Red Barn' (JFS II 208 and 118), 'Henry Martin' (JFS IV 302), 'Fanny Blair' (VW MS but Butterworth version in Dawney, *op.cit.*, p.43), 'The Rambling Sailor' (no 110) and 'Robing Wood and the Pedlar' (JFS II 156); (Mr Peter Verrall) 'Cloddy Banks' (no 105) and 'Merry Green Broomfields' (Bronson, *op.cit.*, pp.110–111, s.n. 'The Squire in the North Country'). In addition, other collectors noted songs from Mrs Verrall (see JFS IV 327 and 281).

104. The Young Servant Man

II 258 (JFS II 98), tune only; Mr and Mrs Verrall; 8 x 1904. Text: broadside no 439, entitled 'The Cruel Father and Affectionate Lovers', printed by J. Harkness, Preston (Madden 18/975).

105. Cloddy Banks

I 263; Mr Verrall; 8 ix 1908. Laws N 40, 'Banks of Claudy'.

106. Cupid the Ploughboy

II 254 (JFS IV 337), tune and first verse; Mr and Mrs Verrall; 8 x 1904. Remainder of text based on broadside printed by W.S. Fortey, Monmouth Court, Seven Dials (Madden 11/748). Laws O 7. 'Cupid's Triumph': RB IV 13.

107. The Lark in the Morning

II 148, tune and text of first verse; Mrs Verrall; 24 v 1904. Remainder of text based on broadside without imprint, entitled 'The Ploughboy' (No 41. Travellers' Vocal Museum, Sold at the Back of No. 10, High Street, Birmingham. Rags taken in, and exchanged: Ballads 119932, p.11, Birmingham Reference Library).

108. The Banks of the Nile

II 140; Mrs Verrall; 24 v 1904. The words, 'my love' have been inserted in a blank left in the MS (v.4, l.1) and 'For' added at the beginning of l.2 (same

[199]

verse). The second half of 1.3 (verse 5) reads in the MS: 'all for the length of time'. Laws N 9.

109. The Gallant *Rainbow*

II 266; Mr and Mrs Verrall; 8 x 1904. Verse 3, l.1 and 2, and v.4, l.3, added.

110. The Rambling Sailor

III 423, tune only; Mr and Mrs Verrall; 2 v 1907. The version given here is, however, the tune (transcribed by Katharine Thomson) and first two verses from a phonograph recording made by VW of Mr Verrall (Tape 267, CSH); remainder of text from version noted from Mr Verrall by George Butterworth in vi 1909 (in Dawney, *op.cit.*, pp.36–7).

111. Duke William

III 277, tune only; Mr Henry Burstow (shoemaker), Horsham, Sussex; xi 1905. Text: in the informant's hand in the scrapbook. Wehse 490, 'Duke William's Frolick'. Henry Burstow (1826–1916) had a repertoire of 420 songs, of which VW noted 33, including 'Through Moorfields', 'The Cheshire Gate', 'Creeping Jane' and 'The Convict's Lamentation' (nos 113, 115, 112 and 114 respectively); and 'Boney's in St Helena', 'Deeds of Napoleon', 'Grand Conversation on Napoleon', 'Pretty Wench', 'North Fleet', '18th Day of June', 'Basket of Eggs', 'The Devil and Ploughman' (JFS II 89, 186, 188, 190, 191, 193, 102 and 184 respectively) and 'Salisbury Plain' (JFS IV 324). Lucy Broadwood and W.H. Gill also collected from him.

112. Creeping Jane

4to I 12; Henry Burstow; 7 xii 1903. VW noted tune and first verse only; remainder of words in Burstow's hand (Scrapbook). Laws Q 23.

113. Through Moorfields

I 403; Henry Burstow; n.d. VW noted the words and tune of the last verse only, from a phonograph recording made in 1907. There are further transcriptions from the same recording, together with a notation made from Burstow in 1893 in Lucy Broadwood, *English Traditional Songs and Carols*, 1908, pp.8–9. Vv.1–8 of the text have been taken from a MS in Burstow's hand in the Broadwood Papers (CSH).

114. The Convict's Lamentation

4to I 13; Henry Burstow, at Leith Hill Place, Surrey; 7 xii 1903. The tune and first four lines are in the hand of VW; full text in the hand of HB, pasted into MS, HB's spelling has been regularised. V.6, ll.1–4 added from H. Anderson, *The Story of Australian Folk Song*, New York, 1970, p.14.

115. The Cheshire Gate

4to I 11, tune only, s.n. 'It was just against the Chasher Gate'; as no 114. Text in HB's hand (Scrapbook). Spelling regularised.

116. An Acre of Land

III 218 (JFS II 212); Mr Frank Bailey, Combe Bissett, Wiltshire; 31 viii 1904. Child 2, 'The Elfin Knight'. Two other songs, including 'Tuesday Morning' (EBECS no 86). For a Yorkshire version, see the title song of *A Yacre of Land* (no 1).

117. Through the Groves
MS wanting (JFS III 285–6); Mr E. Shergold (aged 75), of Amesbury, Wiltshire, at Southampton Workhouse; i 1909. 'Maiden's Complaint': slip song without imprint (Madden 5/1060).
118. Young William
III 6–7; Mr Willy Knaggs, at the *Duncombe Arms*, Westerdale, Yorkshire; 13 vii 1904. V.2 in MS begins: 'Enough (?)'. Vv.4 and 6 added from broadside no 150, entitled 'Kiss me in the Dark', printed by J. Harkness, Preston (Madden 18/680). Wehse 121. Two other songs.
119. I Married a Wife
III 16; Mr John Norton, Robin Hood's Bay, Yorkshire; 22 vii 1904. Two other songs.
120. The Milkmaids
I 59; gypsy, Hooton Roberts, Yorkshire; ix 1907. The first MS verse has been slightly shortened to fit the music; lines 3 and 4 in v.3 have been reversed. Vv.4–7 have been added from broadside printed by Kendrew, Colliergate, York (York Publications, p.29, BL). Three other songs, including 'I Courted an Old Man' (no 121).
121. I Courted an Old Man
I 66; as no 120. Vv.2 and 3 in the MS have been reversed; vv.4–8 have been added from broadside no 87, entitled 'Never Maids Wed an Old Man', printed by Harkness, Preston (Madden 18/174). Wehse 280.

Acknowledgements

I should like to thank: Mrs Ursula Vaughan Williams, not only for her permission to make this selection, but also for her encouragement and help; Mr Malcolm Taylor, of the Vaughan Williams Memorial Library at Cecil Sharp House for his efficient and untiring assistance; and Mr Mike Yates for his generous and valuable advice; also John Connolly, Edith Fowke, Peter Freshwater, Vic Gammon, Keith Gregson, Thomas Gretton, Elizabeth James, A. L. Lloyd, Pat Palmer, Edgar Samuel, Stephen Sedley, Katharine Thomson and Tony Wales. I am also grateful for the assistance of these institutions: Berkshire Record Office, Bodleian Library, Birmingham Reference Library, Birmingham University Library, British Library, British Museum, Cambridge County Record Office, Cambridge University Library, Derby Public Library, Grimsby Public Library, Hereford City Library, Hull Public Library, John Rylands University Library of Manchester, Liverpool Record Office, Mitchell Library (Glasgow), National Maritime Museum, Norfolk Museums Service, Sheffield University Library, St Bride Institute and the Vaughan Williams Memorial Library.

Index of Singers

References are to song numbers

Anderson, Mr 56, 57
Anonymous (a) Barnard Castle, 13,
   14, 15; (b) man from Stepney 81;
   (c) Southwold 87; (d) gypsy 120,
   121
Austin, Mr Jim 6
Bailey, Mr Frank 116
Baines, Mr Ted 96, 97
Bell, Mr 21
Berry, Mrs 88
Bone, Mr William 38, 39
Brice, Mr 77
Broomfield, Mr 19, 20
Brown, Sally 64
Burstow, Mr Henry 111–115
Carruthers, Mr 9, 10, 11
Carter, Mr 53, 54
Chidell, Mrs 29
Clements, Mr David 31
Colcombe, Mr William 45
Copas, Mr 1
Crist, Mr 60–63
Day, Mr Henry 30
Dykes, Mr 51
Earle, Mr 89
Evans, Mr John 42
Fisher, Mr Noah ('Blue') 72, 73
Flack, Mr 'Hoppy' 4, 5
Flint, Mr 90, 91
Garman, Mr 93, 94, 95
Goodyear, Mrs 32
Gothard, Mr 7
Hall, Mr J. 12
Harper, Mr 58, 59
Hilton, Mr 66, 67
Hirons, Mr 43

Howard, Mrs Betty 65
Humphrys, Mrs 17, 18
Hurr, Mr Robert 79, 80
Hurr, Mr William 82
Kemp, Mr 24, 35
Knaggs, Mr W. 118
Leary, Mr 27, 28
Leatherday, Mr 55
Locke, Mr 70, 71
Loveridge, Junior, Mr 50
Lovett, Mr George 33
Morris, Mr 44, 45
Nevill, Mr Ted 26
Norton, Mr John 119
Penfold, Mr David 100, 101, 102
Porter, Mr Alfred 34
Pottipher, Mr Charles 16
Powell, Mrs Ellen 47, 48
Punt, Mr James 22, 23
Saxton, Mr 49
Shergold, Mr E. 117
Smith, Mrs Esther 40, 41
Stacey, Mr 98, 99
Teal, Mr Frederick 92
Thompson, Mr 75, 76
Truell, Mr and Mrs 52
Tuffs, Senior, Mr 69
Verrall, Mr and Mrs 103–110
Waggs, Mr Billy 86
Warner, Mr 78
Wetherill, Mr 2, 3
Whitby, Mr 68
Wigg, Mr Daniel 35, 36, 37
Willis, Mr Jake 83, 84, 85
Wiltshire, Mr 8
Woods, Mr 74

Index of Titles and First Lines

First lines in italics. References are to page numbers.

[205]

[206]